# CREATING AND MANAGING THE FULL-SERVICE HOMEWORK CENTER

# CREATING and MANAGING
# THE FULL-SERVICE HOMEWORK CENTER

WITHDRAWN

Cindy Mediavilla

ala editions

An imprint of the American Library Association
Chicago \ 2018

**CINDY MEDIAVILLA** is the author of *Creating the Full-Service Homework Center in Your Library* (ALA, 2001), which has been called "the quintessential guide to the practicalities of setting up a formal homework help center to provide one-to-one homework assistance to student patrons" (Intner, *Homework Help from the Library*, ix). In the early 1990s Mediavilla managed a homework center, called the Friendly Stop, for the Orange (CA) Public Library, and she has been studying after-school homework programs ever since. She has published several articles on the topic and has evaluated homework programs for the Long Beach and Los Angeles public libraries. She has made presentations on homework help programs at the conferences of several major library associations, and she has also conducted many workshops on the topic. A former public librarian for eighteen years, Mediavilla has both an MLS degree and a doctorate in library science from UCLA.

ISBN: 978-0-8389-1618-6 (paper)

**Library of Congress Cataloging-in-Publication Data**
Names: Mediavilla, Cindy, 1953- author.
Title: Creating and managing the full-service homework center / Cindy Mediavilla.
Description: Chicago : ALA Editions, 2018. | Includes bibliographical references and index.
Identifiers: LCCN 2017024319 | ISBN 9780838916186 (paperback : alk. paper)
Subjects: LCSH: Homework centers in libraries—United States. | Libraries and students—United States. | Homework—United States—Library resources.
Classification: LCC Z718.7 .M435 2018 | DDC 025.50973—dc23 LC record available at https://lccn
    .loc.gov/2017024319

Book design by Alejandra Diaz in the Mrs Eaves XL Serif Nar and Benton Sans Compressed typefaces.

♾ This paper meets the requirements of ANSI/NISO Z39.48-1992 (Permanence of Paper).

Printed in the United States of America
22  21  20  19  18      5  4  3  2  1

# CONTENTS

*Acknowledgments / vii*
*Introduction / ix*

| ONE | **Why Homework Centers?** | 1 |
| TWO | **Community Assessment** | 7 |
| THREE | **Service Plan** | 13 |
| FOUR | **Staff and Volunteer Recruitment** | 19 |
| FIVE | **Job Duties and Training** | 25 |
| SIX | **Funding and Partnerships** | 31 |
| SEVEN | **Collaboration with Schools** | 35 |
| EIGHT | **Space and Location** | 39 |
| NINE | **Service Hours** | 43 |
| TEN | **Programming and Corollary Services** | 47 |

ELEVEN **Library Resources** 51

TWELVE **Supplies and Equipment** 59

THIRTEEN **Security, User Expectations, and Rules of Conduct** 63

FOURTEEN **Media and Public Relations** 69

FIFTEEN **Evaluation and Measuring Outcomes** 73

*Appendixes*

   A   Model Homework Programs / 82
   B   Community Assessment Tools / 95
   C   Homework Staff Recruitment Announcements / 98
   D   Homework Helper Application Forms / 101
   E   Homework Helper Contract / 105
   F   Homework Staff Job Descriptions / 107
   G   Training Modules / 117
   H   Staff Manual Excerpts / 127
   I   Letter of Intent / 131
   J   Teacher Letters / 132
   K   Registration Forms / 134
   L   Survey Instruments / 138

*Bibliography* / *159*
*Index* / *163*

# ACKNOWLEDGMENTS

Even though I've studied homework center programs for more than twenty-five years, I'm still thrilled every time I walk into a public library after school and see either adults or peers helping kids with their schoolwork. I am so grateful to former Orange Public Library director Karen Leo for hiring me in 1991 to, among other things, oversee the Friendly Stop, a grant-funded homework center located in the heart of a Latino barrio. Little did I know that my entire professional outlook would change when I took that job. I also remain extremely indebted to professor emerita Virginia Walter, whose love of children and libraries continues to inspire my own passion for public service. You are a wonderful mentor and friend.

I also want to thank ALA acquisitions editor Jamie Santoro, who encouraged me to submit a proposal to update my original homework centers book, published sixteen years ago. Your support through the research and writing process is greatly appreciated. Many thanks, too, to the UCLA Office of Academic Personnel for awarding me a non-senate faculty professional development grant to support my travel to homework centers in Washington State and throughout California.

As I did for my first book, I visited many homework help programs—virtually as well as in person—during my research. I could not have written this book without the help of Mari Hardacre, Allen County Public Library, Indiana; Amanda Bressler and Barbara A. Rhodes, Boston Public Library; Jack Rothstein, Brainfuse; Elizabeth McChesney, Chicago Public Library; Debbie Anderson, County of Los Angeles Public Library; Julia Boxler, Cuyahoga County Public Library, Ohio; Kari Evans, Gwinnett County Library, Georgia; Katherine Debertin, Hennepin County Library, Minnesota; Annie Poyner, King County Library System, Washington; Katherine Merrell, Lafayette Public Library, Colorado; Imani Harris, Library Foundation of Los Angeles; Cynthia Bautista, Long Beach Public Library, California; Madeline Bryant and Candice Mack, Los Angeles Public Library; Sarah Stimson, Mission Viejo Library, California; Christopher Hosler and Jan Pierson, Monroe County Library, Indiana; Be Astengo, Monterey County Free Libraries, California; Jill Patterson, OC Public Libraries, California; Michael Barb, Palos Verdes Library District, California; Melissa Bailey and Karen Christiansen, Paso Robles Public Library, California; Chris Caputo and Heather Sparks, Free Library of Philadelphia; Alice Johnson Bisanz, Prospect Heights Public Library, Illinois; Katherine McMillan, Sacramento Public Library; Eric Whalen, Saint Paul Public Library, Minnesota; Marina Claudio-Perez, Danielle Ghio, and Haley Zamora, San Diego

Public Library; Mark Giannuzzi and Jason Pell, San José Public Library, California; Kelly Behle, Santa Clarita Public Library, California; Dawn Jackson and Vickie Gill, Santa Maria Public Library, California; Nancy Garrett and Josie Watanabe, Seattle Public Library; Kevin Tolley, Solano County Library, California; Julia Albright and Susan Mikula, Ventura County Library, California; and Jasmine Andrews and Toni Mendieta, Yolo County Library, California.

Finally, I want to thank my husband Tim Ahern for always supporting my many projects, even when they inevitably lead to predawn mornings and late nights. I'm so happy that you're able to travel with me when I go on my various research trips. Someday I, too, will truly retire!

**CINDY MEDIAVILLA**
APRIL 2017

# INTRODUCTION

In 2001 the American Library Association (ALA) published my book *Creating the Full-Service Homework Center in Your Library*. Three years earlier, I had applied for and received an ALA Loleta D. Fyan Grant to study homework assistance programs throughout the country. At the time, formal "homework centers" were still a relatively new phenomenon in public libraries, even though librarians had, of course, been helping students with their schoolwork for many decades. Motivated by my own career-changing experience overseeing the Friendly Stop, an after-school homework center at the Orange Public Library in California, I was convinced my research would uncover four or five models that others could replicate. Instead, I found that every program reflected the distinct needs of its unique community. Despite some shared commonalities, each library offered homework services that were often decidedly different from the rest. My 2001 book aimed to bring these various models together in hopes of inspiring other libraries to create their own homework help programs.

Since then, after-school homework help has become a mainstream service offered in many public libraries nationwide. In its most recent *Public Library Service Responses*, the Public Library Association (PLA) includes "Succeed in School: Homework Help" as one of eighteen strategies for responding to community needs. Using concise bullet points, the authors outline the following elements to consider when helping students succeed in school:

> policies
> critical resources (i.e., staff knowledge and skills, collection, facilities, and technology)
> potential partners
> service measurement (Garcia and Nelson 2007)

Even more recently, the ALA's Reference User Services Association (RUSA) and Young Adult Library Services Association (YALSA) solicited their members' input on how to maximize in-library homework assistance. Respondents identified several obstacles to providing homework help in the library, including the lack of space, lack of qualified staff and other helpers, and poor communication with school personnel. When asked how homework help might be provided despite the lack of library resources, librarians pointed to the need for grant funding, trained volunteers, and a list of authoritative but free educational websites. Despite perceived barriers, the majority of respondents agreed that the ALA should nonetheless encourage libraries to provide after-school homework help. As a result, a joint RUSA/YALSA committee compiled a list of "Homework Help Best Practices" that includes tips on needs assessment, partnerships, policies, promotion, designated space, staffing, schedules, collections, evaluation, and funding (YALSA Board of Directors Meeting 2015). Perhaps not so coincidentally, YALSA has also recently listed studying "the impact of libraries as teen formal and informal learning environments" as the first priority on its national research agenda for 2017 through 2021.[1]

## EVOLVING SERVICES

Although my first book has been called "the quintessential guide to the practicalities of setting up a formal homework help center" (Intner 2011, ix), the methods for assisting students in their academic endeavors have evolved over the past fifteen years. Most notably, synchronous homework help is now accessible online through many public libraries. In 2001, the California State Library conducted a series of teen focus groups statewide, soliciting input on desired library services. In addition to longer hours and a more welcoming environment, young people specified the need for after-school homework assistance. Thus California became the first state to offer online tutoring via public libraries statewide (Minkel 2002). Today, online homework help provided by vendors, like Tutor.com and Brainfuse, is ubiquitous in libraries throughout the United States.

Moreover, many public library after-school programs have moved beyond just offering homework help. Philadelphia's formerly homework-heavy Literacy Enrichment After-School Program (LEAP), for instance, has evolved into an award-winning out-of-school time service that grooms future leaders as well as productive students. In Long Beach, California, the library's Family Learning Centers provide both makerspaces and computers for completing schoolwork, while homework helpers at libraries in Minneapolis and King County, Washington, are encouraged to assist students with submitting college and scholarship applications. For some public libraries, homework help is only one part of an overall philosophy supporting student success.

While much of my first book is still relevant, I have updated the content by contacting and, in some cases, visiting several stellar public library homework sites around the country. Some of these programs, like those in Monterey County, California, and Seattle have been tested over the years and are still providing a vitally needed service. Others are relatively new. Though no two of these are exactly alike, they all share a desire to help young people succeed and so are model programs in their own right. I am also happy to report that many of the libraries cited in this book used my first book to inform how they currently deliver after-school homework services.

## ABOUT THIS BOOK

In my first book, I identified three main elements critical to all effective homework centers: (1) staff or volunteers who are trained to help young people with their schoolwork; (2) space designated for student use during specific days and times; and (3) a multi-format collection of school-related materials (Mediavilla 2001, x). While trained helpers and adequate space continue to be essential components of successful homework programs, the need for traditional library materials to support school assignments has come into question. In a thought-provoking YALSA blog post, Sarah Ludwig and Linda W. Braun (2011b) argue that the focus of library homework help should move "from collections (physical and web-based)" to "space, hours, flexible technology, and human support"—in other words, less content and more facilitation. After all, as "public geek" Phil Shapiro (2017) has observed, many students just need a place to access the technological resources they lack at home. Nevertheless, Common Core State Standards and other curricular innovations dictate the need for primary and additional written data. Therefore, it is incumbent that public libraries continue to offer traditional materials as well as access to advanced technology and online resources.

Based on these new homework help factors, I have updated my definition of a *full-service homework center* as a program dedicated to meeting the curricular needs of students by providing

> staff or volunteers who are trained to assist students with their homework
> space designated for student use during specific days and times
> a variety of library resources, including up-to-date technology, print materials, and online sites that help facilitate the completion of school assignments

Like the earlier version, this book is organized according to the several elements necessary to provide effective homework assistance. Included in this book are chapters discussing

> community assessment
> service plans
> staff and volunteer recruitment
> job duties and training
> funding and partnerships
> collaboration with schools
> space and location
> service hours
> programming and corollary services
> library resources
> supplies and equipment
> security, user expectations, and rules of conduct
> media and public relations
> evaluation and measuring outcomes

Each chapter includes a short "talking points" sidebar that highlights critical factors relative to homework centers and that chapter's topic. The points give readers something to ponder as well as ammunition when arguing in favor of creating a homework help program.

In the appendixes, I have assembled real-life

> community assessment tools
> homework center staff recruitment announcements, job descriptions, applications, and contracts
> excerpts from homework center staff manuals
> sample letters to teachers
> program registration forms
> sample survey instruments

The book also profiles ten exemplary homework programs that represent a wide range of organizational and funding scenarios (see appendix A). Included here are single-outlet centers as well as multibranch programs that serve large cities, such as Los Angeles and Chicago. Some of these programs have been completely absorbed into their library's service priorities and budgets, while others still rely on the generosity of foundations and outside funders. And although most homework centers tend to help students from mostly low-income or immigrant neighborhoods, at least one model program is flourishing in an upscale, middle-class community.

My hope is that readers will be able to "mix and match" the relevant aspects of all the programs described in this book to create and manage even more unique homework center models, based on their own community priorities.

## NOTE

1. YALSA National Research Agenda, www.ala.org/yalsa/guidelines/research/researchagenda.

# WHY HOMEWORK CENTERS?

HOMEWORK TYPICALLY CONSISTS OF TASKS THAT STUDENTS ARE expected to complete during non-school hours. Assignments may range anywhere from tabulating simple fractions to explicating an Emily Dickinson poem to creating a conceptual mock-up of an international space station. In most cases, homework reinforces student learning, while encouraging creativity and deeper exploration. School assignments provide opportunities for collaborative problem-solving as well as independent thinking and may help build organizational and time-management skills. In other words, homework serves many purposes in a student's life.

As the educational psychologist Pamela Warton (2001) notes, however, even the most well-intentioned assignments can be a source of considerable stress and conflict. Many call this phenomenon the "homework wars"—that is, the challenges that lead to strife rather than positive learning and often cause contentious situations at home. Today's parents don't always know what their children are studying, nor do they necessarily have the time, energy, or skills to help their kids learn to read or do math. Moreover, low-income families may not have access to the sophisticated resources required to excel in school. Combine this with a home environment where English is a second language, and the child has no alternative but to seek homework help elsewhere.

Youngsters may also need a safe place to go once school ends. In 1992, the Carnegie Council on Adolescent Development famously concluded that the most dangerous time of day for youth is the three hours following school. This is when kids are most susceptible to bad influences and are more liable to engage in illegal activities. To address the situation, the council recommended creating after-school programs that provide safe shelter, as well as positive learning experiences, and admonished community leaders, including librarians, to serve as change agents. Several years later, a federal study found that youngsters who participate in after-school programs not only tend to succeed academically, but also develop stronger social skills and learn how to acceptably handle conflict. According to the report, after-school programs should foster meaningful relationships between young people and caring adults, while building partnerships with families, schools, and the community. Effective programs are those that also provide enriching learning activities and a safe and healthy after-school environment (U.S. Department of Education and U.S. Department of Justice 2000). Subsequent studies by the After-school Alliance, the California Afterschool Network, the Harvard Family Research Project, and the American Policy Youth Forum have yielded similar findings and recommendations.[1]

## STUDENTS AND PUBLIC LIBRARIES

Like many relationships, the dynamic between school kids and libraries is sometimes strained. Though early twentieth-century public librarians welcomed students with open arms, by the 1950s their reception was far less enthusiastic as young baby boomers began inundating libraries after school. Cold War competition with the Soviet Union exacerbated the situation as a renewed emphasis on academic success became paramount, further taxing institutional resources. Librarians everywhere struggled to manage what many called "the student problem." Some public libraries even required use permits from parents or teachers, while others restricted services altogether. As Margaret A. Edwards (1969) remarked in her classic book *A Fair Garden and the Swarm of Beasts*, not only did librarians make young people feel unwanted, they also made them feel ignorant.

Unfortunately, this antagonism between libraries and students has, in some cases, lingered. In a study cited by Melissa Gross (2000), high school graduates classified librarians into three types: those who like to point, those who like to help, and those who hate young people. Likewise, Elaine Meyers (1999) discovered that many teens think librarians prefer books to kids. In a study of early library chat services, Virginia Walter and I observed that virtual librarians quickly referred students to an online tutoring service, instead of answering homework questions themselves (Walter and Mediavilla 2005). According to Don Sager (1997), the "blackboard curtain" often descends as soon as students approach library staff and ask for homework help.

Although some librarians may still feel that curriculum-based programs are best left to the schools, others understand just how interrelated academic and public library services are. Formal after-school homework help programs began emerging in public libraries as early as the 1980s. In National City, California, Project My Turn, a joint public library and local school program, paired junior-high kids with high school-aged tutors to help students strengthen their literacy and homework-related skills (Dunmore and

### TALKING POINTS

Not everyone is convinced that public libraries should offer formal homework help programs. When arguing in favor of providing homework assistance in the library, emphasize the following:

- Research has shown that children and teens need a safe place to go after school, as this is the most dangerous time of day for youth. Homework centers provide students with a supportive environment where they can engage in positive educational activities.

- Unlike the campus, where after-school programs often connote remedial learning or detention, students feel welcome in public libraries because they are less restrictive and because they provide the resources needed to do homework.

- Evidence overwhelmingly confirms that public library homework programs result in positive outcomes, including better homework comprehension, improved grades, improved after-school behaviors and study habits, better communication skills, and enriched relationships.

Hardiman 1987). At the other end of the state, the Seaside branch offered one of the first official homework "centers" to manage unsupervised latchkey children who raised havoc in the library every day after school (Brewer 1992). Seaside's program eventually spread to branches throughout the system and is now an important part of Monterey County Free Libraries' after-school service. Other long-standing library homework help programs can be found in Hennepin County, Minnesota; King County, Washington; Philadelphia; Seattle; Ventura County, California; and Lafayette, Colorado.

## BENEFITS OF HOMEWORK HELP PROGRAMS

At the very least, the library's homework center provides students with a designated place to go after school. At its best, the program offers positive human interaction and scholastic support that might otherwise be missing from a youngster's life. While on-campus after-school programs may be negatively associated with remedial learning or detention, homework-friendly public libraries are more "cool" because they offer an educationally conducive and flexible environment in which to study. Not only do public libraries provide space, staff, and resources, they're also open year-round and are accessible during weekends and evenings. Where else can students find reliable information they need *when* they need it?

Over the years, evidence has overwhelmingly confirmed that public library homework programs result in positive benefits. A study of the County of Los Angeles Public Library's homework centers revealed that students view the library as a productive place to complete schoolwork. Youngsters also expressed appreciation for library staff who take the time to explain assignments and help them understand what their teachers expect. In addition, 72 percent of parents surveyed said their children come home with more complete homework after attending the library's center (Bailey 1999). An evaluation of the Cuyahoga County Public Library's homework program, in Ohio, yielded even more robust results, with 100 percent of participants' parents saying their children now understand their homework better. Seventy-nine percent also indicated that their kids' grades had improved as a result of getting homework help at the library, while another 79 percent said their children now spend more time doing homework (Huffman and Rua 2008). More recently, 87 percent of homework-help participants in Chicago said they felt better about school as a result of attending the Teacher in the Library program. Ninety-five percent of parents concurred, saying their children now have a better attitude about schoolwork ("Teacher in the Library Survey Results" 2014).

Young people's after-school behaviors improve as well. The staff of a library located within walking distance of a middle school and high school in Gwinnett County, Georgia, dealt with several challenging after-school situations until the branch manager decided to start a homework center for teens. Although the program is relatively new, staff have already noticed a positive change in the atmosphere after school because the kids, who use the homework center, now demonstrate more productive behavior. One tenth grader even improved her math grade by fifteen points, from a low C to a B. Several students have also become repeat customers of the library.

Other benefits also abound. An early evaluation of the Monterey County Free Libraries' program confirmed that not only do participants improve their study habits, they also gain confidence and interpersonal skills. Users learned how to advocate for themselves in school and became classroom role models for other students. In addition, the library's program helped build collaborative skills by encouraging kids to work with their friends (Brown 2002). Indeed, an ALA-sponsored investigation of teen-focused homework centers showed that teamwork naturally evolves as young people study together. By focusing on their schoolwork, students set an example for others and become positive role models. A high standard of behavior is expected in library homework centers where good manners and patience are rewarded (Walter and Mediavilla 2003; Walter and Meyers 2003).

Communication skills also tend to improve as young people learn to articulate their school needs. Immigrant children may even improve their English language skills. In Minneapolis, for instance, homework helpers have been instrumental in helping Somali youngsters acclimate to their new home. "I couldn't speak a word of English when I came here three years ago," one high school student told me. "And now look at me! I'll be going to college in the fall, thanks to the library!"

Students may also develop meaningful relationships with homework helpers. In the library, young people have the opportunity to see adults in a nonclassroom, nonparental role. Most students appreciate the assistance they receive and understand that, in many cases, these adults are volunteering their time to help kids succeed in school. One mother said her daughter feels important when the library's homework helper, a retired engineer, tutors her in math (Walter and Mediavilla 2003). And of course, younger kids love getting help from high school and college students. Teenaged homework helpers often bring hope and encouragement to neighborhoods where few positive role models exist. They also prove that succeeding in school is possible. As one program coordinator explained, sometimes tutors become mentors.

Helping young people succeed in school can be very rewarding for the helpers, too. A retired teacher in San Diego provides homework help in the library because she wants to enrich children's minds. Another helper, a retired administrator in Sacramento, revels in seeing youngsters' "eyes light up" when they suddenly understand their homework. Likewise, a grandmother in King County said she enjoys seeing students grow mentally as well as physically. "It's a lot more fun helping other kids do their homework than it was helping my own daughters," she joked.

Young people also welcome the opportunity to assist fellow students. Teens in low-income and ethnic neighborhoods, in particular, often express a keen sense of "giving back" to their communities. Younger helpers are grateful for the skills gained as a result of providing homework assistance, while the more ambitious ones view this experience as a résumé-builder or a plus for their college application. In Yolo County, California, a high school senior, who has participated in the library's homework program since eighth grade, said he originally wanted to become a police officer, but is now considering a career in political science after listening to children's concerns for so many years. Other helpers often decide they are best suited to become teachers or pediatric nurses. One young man even realized he would be a good father. Helping kids with their homework can be a life-changing experience.

**NOTE**

1. Research on the effectiveness of after-school programs is continuously being conducted and published by the Afterschool Alliance, www.afterschoolalliance.org/researchAfterschool Essentials.cfm; the California Afterschool Network, www.afterschoolnetwork.org/after-school-research; the Harvard Family Research Project, www.hfrp.org/; and the American Policy Youth Forum, www.aypf.org/programareas/afterschoolexpanded-learning, among others.

# COMMUNITY ASSESSMENT

PUBLIC LIBRARIES OFFER FORMAL HOMEWORK HELP FOR MANY REASONS. In one of the earliest articles about such programs, Rosellen Brewer (1992) tells how she was inspired to start her library's after-school center while attending a workshop on multiculturalism. Listening to the speakers, she began asking herself several poignant questions: How many students don't go to class because they haven't finished their homework? How many don't finish their homework because there is no one to help them or because they can't find a quiet place to study? If parents are willing to leave their children in the library as a method of day care, how sensitive can they be to their kids' homework needs? Pondering possible answers to these questions, Brewer decided that the public library is the best place to help students do their schoolwork.

In La Habra, California, an after-school homework help program was started at the urging of a high school student who served on the library's teen advisory board and volunteered with Families for Literacy. She noticed that there were literacy services for preschoolers and adults, but nothing was available for the elementary school students who gathered in the library every afternoon. And so, in 2003, the La Habra branch of OC Public Libraries, in Orange County, launched the Homework Help Teen Tutor program that's still going strong today ("La Habra Branch Library Teen Tutors" 2006).

External forces may also motivate the creation of library homework centers. Programs in Whittier, California, and San Diego began after government officials offered the library discretionary funds to develop after-school activities for kids. In Fort Wayne, Indiana, a citizen's panel report on youth, violence, and high dropout rates eventually convinced the library to provide a program where teens could get homework help in the evening. Likewise, low class attendance prompted the Cuyahoga County Public Library, in Ohio, to look for ways to help students stay in school. In response, the children's librarian at the Maple Heights branch began offering formal homework assistance in the afternoon (Huffman and Rua 2008). Today Cuyahoga's program has expanded to ten sites countywide.

Although some homework centers thrive under a "build-it-and-they-will-come" model, the most successful programs are those that are created directly in response to community need. Indeed, in their joint "Homework Help Best Practices" statement, the Reference User Services Association and the Young Adult Library Services Association list "needs assessment" as the first of several elements to consider when developing homework programs for teens (YALSA Board of Directors Meeting 2015). Sarah Ludwig and Linda W. Braun (2011a) further elaborate, admonishing public libraries to check with teens first to see if they even want or need homework support. "Without teen input," they insist, "librarians may find themselves spinning their wheels, spending money and staff time on materials and programs that are underused, and building [homework help] websites that are rarely visited."

## TALKING POINTS

Although some homework centers thrive under a "build-it-and-they-will-come" model, the most successful programs are those that are created in direct response to community need. Few libraries take the time to assess their communities, however. Therefore, when convincing staff and administrators of the need for community assessment, be sure to emphasize that:

- Soliciting direct input from the target population is more effective than drawing conclusions based on professional knowledge or random observation. The best community assessments make use of both expert and public knowledge.

- Environmental scans are a relatively easy way to create a demographic snapshot of the community. In planning a homework help program, it's important to assess the target population's technology levels as well as languages spoken.

- Surveys and interviews are efficient methods of gathering community input. To be effective, questionnaires should be brief, free of technical or library jargon, written in a language respondents understand, and easy to return.

## ASSESSMENT METHODS

In our book *5 Steps of Outcome-Based Planning and Evaluation for Public Libraries*, Melissa Gross, Virginia Walter, and I use a hypothetical case study to reinforce the process required to plan and carry out effective library programs. Our scenario starts when, as a result of talking to local parents and teachers, library staff learn that many middle school students are failing math. To address the issue, the library brings together a team of community members and staff to develop a strategy to help middle school students understand their math homework. They ultimately accomplish their goal by offering an after-school math-tutoring program in the library. Though our case study is fictional, the message here is very real: programs are most likely to succeed only after taking the important first step of identifying community priorities (Gross, Mediavilla, and Walter 2016).

As practitioners, librarians often rely on what the Harwood Institute for Public Innovation (2016) calls "expert knowledge"— that is, the knowledge that comes from education, professional analysis, market studies, and best practices. This is different from "public knowledge" that comes directly from community members. James Corburn (2005) calls this more local form of information "street knowledge," where community members understand the realities of daily life far better than outsiders do. Local knowledge manifests itself in conversations and direct input from the community, while expert knowledge is validated through study and peer review. The best community assessments incorporate both types of input.

There are several ways to assess one's community, including environmental scans, literature review, observation, and, of course, direct input from surveys and conversations. Some of these techniques may be familiar, some may not; but when conducted thoughtfully and intentionally, these methods can be quite effective at eliciting the aspirations and concerns of potential homework center users. Utilizing a combination of these techniques ensures that both public- and expert-knowledge-based input is considered when designing the library's homework center.

## ENVIRONMENTAL SCANS AND LITERATURE REVIEW

The best place to start is an environmental scan, where as much information as possible is gathered about successful homework programs and the library's options for offering such a service. Searching for articles in the relevant literature, both within and outside the library profession, should come quite naturally to staff. Reading this book, for example, is an obvious first step to researching the various aspects of creating and managing a formal homework help program. But what has happened in the field since the literature's publication? Moreover, what are the new trends in education? Has the local school district instituted any curricular changes that might impact homework help in the library? And who else is offering formal homework assistance in the community? Although the Seattle Public Library and its neighboring system in King County happily welcome community requests for new homework center sites, neither library proceeds until the actual need is investigated and established. When resources are limited, not all requests for new homework centers are filled. In fact, RUSA and YALSA recommend providing resources to local homework help agencies rather than duplicating those efforts in the library (YALSA Board of Directors Meeting 2015, 2).

Librarians should also study local demographics to determine who might need the most homework assistance and at what level. The teacher and experienced tutor Carol F. Intner (2011) contends that Latino and African American students may have more need for library computers than their white or Asian counterparts. In addition, she recommends making note of languages spoken in the community, since this may indicate a need for homework helpers who are fluent in languages other than English.

## OBSERVATION

As helpful as literature reviews and environmental scans can be, it is often first-hand observation that provides the most powerful impetus for launching a new program. Brewer (1992) may have had an epiphany about kids' homework needs while attending a workshop on multiculturalism, but her own eyes reminded her of a much more pressing problem once she returned to the library. A large number of unattended children occupied her branch every day, causing a chronic "latchkey" situation after school. By offering formal homework assistance, Brewer not only helped kids meet their academic needs, she also gave them a purpose for visiting the library, instead of running around and causing havoc in the stacks.

While staff can certainly attest to the fact that the library is inundated every day with students needing help, not all homework activity happens in the library. Whenever possible, librarians should make a point of observing young people in their natural settings. Although the librarian's presence might change the kids' behavior, observation is an easy yet effective assessment technique where one intentionally watches actions as they happen. Observers take note of what they see and then analyze the data to identify the patterns and trends in everyday activities. In Chicago, for instance, public library staff made "outreach visits" into high schools and parks, where they learned that youngsters primarily needed a place to work away from siblings.

## DIRECT INPUT

After observing thousands of students coming into the Brooklyn Public Library for homework help, librarian Barbara Auerbach (1998) decided to survey teens to learn exactly what type of assistance they needed. When she discovered that a great majority of them—84 percent—required math help, the library decided to offer a math peer-tutoring service after school. Soliciting direct input from the target population provided more specific information than mere observations ever could.

Surveys are usually conducted as questionnaires or interviews and are relatively inexpensive to administer. Most libraries use surveys to evaluate services, but they can also be used to assess community aspirations and concerns. In 2013, a stalwart group of residents on the west end of California's Santa Ynez Valley launched a campaign to reopen the Los Alamos library, a small branch of the Santa Maria Public Library that had closed twenty-five years earlier. To rally support and gather evidence of need, the newly formed Friends group interviewed school officials, as well as community members, and discovered that 50 percent of families living closest to the library had no Internet access at home. In addition, the nearby school principal and teachers indicated a need for homework help, especially among the 75 percent of students who speak only Spanish at home. Three months after the branch reopened in 2015, a formal homework help program was started, offering one-on-one tutoring after school.

In planning a homework center, Sian Brannon and WyLaina Hildreth (2011) recommend talking to and surveying students, parents, and teachers regarding their expectations for the program. Questions may include: What types of homework are being assigned and in which subjects? What types of resources (e.g., reference materials, homework helpers, textbooks, computers) would be most helpful? And in which subjects do students need help? Surveys should be brief, free of technical or library jargon, and written in a language respondents understand. Questionnaires should also be easy to return either online, via mail, or to a box inside the library. (For sample survey instruments, please see appendix B.)

After learning that the city of Fort Wayne's dropout rate was on the rise, staff from the Allen County's main library decided to conduct a study to determine the feasibility of providing homework help to teens. Questionnaires were mailed to young adult summer reading club participants and were distributed at schools, youth centers, and inside the library. More than 900 completed questionnaires were collected. Of these, 81 percent indicated a need for homework assistance, with 56 percent saying they would use a homework center if offered. Armed with these data, library staff then interviewed representatives from local homework-support agencies to see if there was an overlap in programs. They also led a focus-group discussion with twenty-two teens. The data collected through all these methods not only helped staff design the homework center, the information also convinced funders of the need. Twenty years later, the Fort Wayne library still offers homework help to teens three nights a week, continuing to meet a vital community need.

# SERVICE PLAN

ECAUSE EACH PROGRAM REFLECTS THE NEEDS OF ITS PARTICULAR community, no two homework centers are exactly alike. Even within the same library system, programs may differ from branch to branch due to unique circumstances and individual community needs. Therefore, a written plan is necessary to describe the exact role the library plays as a homework assistance provider.

## DEFINING PURPOSE

Many public libraries, large and small, include in their mission statement a promise to promote learning and meet the educational needs of the community. The Los Angeles Public Library, for instance, "provides free and easy access to information, ideas, books and technology that enrich, educate and empower every individual in [the] city's diverse communities."[1] Likewise, part of the Boston Public Library's mission is "to serve the cultural, educational, and informational needs of the people of the City and the Commonwealth."[2] In Hennepin County, Minnesota, the library exists to "nourish minds, transform lives and build community together."[3] It also strives to "ensure every person has the opportunity and resources to read, graduate, engage, work and learn." Even the small Santa Clarita Public Library in California strives to "bring people, information, and ideas together to educate, inspire and enrich the quality of life in our diverse Community."[4] The emphasis on education and learning in each of these statements demonstrates a commitment to supporting the community's curricular needs and lays a strong foundation on which to build a homework help program.

From the mission statement come the library's goals and service objectives. If curricular support is to be integrated into the institution's services, then a policy for achieving such a goal should be included in the library's work plan. Hennepin's after-school homework program directly reflects the overall mission of the library. Specifically, the program's goals are to support positive academic outcomes by

> helping students complete homework assignments
> encouraging the development of learning skills, such as problem-solving, critical thinking, and basic literacy and mathematical thinking
> boosting confidence, motivation, and momentum to learn (Hennepin County Library 2016a)

The same is true for the Chicago Public Library, which develops several annual goals for its after-school Teacher in the Library program. The goals for 2016 include

> improve after-school learning habits for school-aged children
> provide a safe and supportive after-school learning environment for children
> help children develop social and communication skills
> encourage positive relationships between children and adults (teachers, parents, and librarians)
> serve as a resource for parents who wish to help their children with homework ("TIL/Homework Help Logic Model" 2016)

From these goals then are listed the inputs—for example, staff, supplies, equipment—plus anticipated activities, including homework assistance sessions, informal parent help, teacher follow-up, and educational games facilitation, that are needed to accomplish the goals. The expectation, of course, is that these efforts will result in a series of benefits that are stated as formal outcomes. The goals, in this case, lead directly to increased homework completion, improved social and communication skills, improved attitudes toward homework and after-school learning, and students' increased confidence in themselves as learners.

In Saint Paul, Minnesota, not only is it the public library's mission to "connect people . . . with the imperative and the joy of learning through a lifetime," but its first strategic goal is to "advance Saint Paul's learning priorities," including "student success in school and life."[5] This focus has, in turn, led to the creation and long-term maintenance of a formal homework help program offered in six branches. The Monterey County Free Libraries, in California, has taken this planning process a step further by creating a mission statement specifically for its homework help program, promising "to help students develop effective study and social skills through active library use." From here, the library has developed four goals, predicting that students who visit their local homework center will

1. Develop effective study skills
2. Become active library users
3. Develop positive relationships with peers and adults
4. Understand and display appropriate library behavior ("Homework Center Goals" 2014)

The accomplishment of these goals—or outcomes—is then used to measure the effectiveness of the program, as discussed in chapter 15.

## SERVICE LEVELS

Although most public library homework programs are rather easy to create and manage, some are far more complicated, employing certified staff at several sites, and providing expensive computer equipment and a robust schedule of homework help hours. Some libraries even offer multiple levels of homework assistance based on the target audiences they hope to attract. For example, the Lafayette Public Library in Colorado provides general homework help for all ages, four afternoons a week, on the library's lower level, while math and physics tutoring is offered exclusively to high schoolers in the group study room upstairs. The math tutors upstairs have specific skills and knowledge not required of the more general homework helpers downstairs. Meanwhile, at the Cuyahoga County Public Library, three distinct programs are offered: structured homework centers, scheduled during specific hours in ten branches; "123 Read," an after-school reading-skills program, run in conjunction with the homework centers, but open only to students who are referred by the school district; and a Homework Mentor program, where helpers rove through the library, approaching students who might need assistance. Libraries will want to carefully consider what level of homework help is most appropriate for their student constituents.

Intner (2011) argues that not all libraries are equipped to offer resource-intensive homework programs. Instead, they may choose to provide less formal options, such as

> small collections of reference titles and basic school supplies
> binders filled with assignments from nearby schools
> textbooks
> computers reserved after school for "homework only"
> regular library staff who are trained and willing to help kids with their schoolwork

She advises libraries to consider what they hope to accomplish by supporting students' schoolwork and then proceed from there. Depending on community needs, different levels of homework help services might focus on

> information literacy
> culturally sensitive instruction
> access to technology
> access to both print and online reference materials
> research skills
> general study skills
> completion of daily school assignments
> academic achievement
> reference services
> a safe after-school environment (Intner 2011, 29–35)

The Public Library Association (PLA) also provides guidance on the various levels of homework help a library might want to offer. In its still-relevant "Succeed in School: Homework Help" service response, the PLA lists an array of potential activities to meet student needs:

> › Provide staff or volunteers to help students with their homework
> › Develop and maintain a homework help web page
> › Provide homework assistance via text messaging
> › Subscribe to an online homework help tutoring service
> › Provide study rooms
> › Provide classroom collections for teachers
> › Work closely with school staff to identify curricular priorities
> › Work with school staff to create an assignment alert program
> › Provide access to distance education or video-on-demand courses
> › Visit school classes
> › Invite school classes to tour the library
> › Provide services specifically for home-schooled students

The PLA also reminds libraries of the policy implications of launching a homework program. How much homework help should staff provide? Are students allowed to work in groups and, if so, are there certain rules they must follow? Should the circulation of homework-related materials be limited? And who is going to staff the homework program? If volunteers, then what are their preferred qualifications and should they be screened? These are all important issues to consider when deciding what level of homework help the library wants to provide (Garcia and Nelson 2007, 54–56).

Once the service level is defined and the program launched, the library should publicly state the homework center's purpose in order to avoid creating false expectations. Usually this is done via the library's website under the youth services banner. Not only is this a good place to describe what the program does, but it also provides the perfect opportunity to clarify what the homework center does not do. On its website, the Los Angeles Public Library explains that its Student Zones provide a quiet and safe study area as well as a place to access resources, such as online and print materials, free printing, basic school supplies, and computer equipment and software. But the site also very specifically warns that "Student Zone Helpers, volunteers and librarians do not provide one-on-one tutoring." Furthermore, the library clearly states that "results are not guaranteed."[6] In King County, Washington, the library's website defines its after-school program as "a place for students to study, do homework, and get help with their questions from volunteer tutors." However, the library "cannot guarantee intensive, private one-on-one tutoring."[7]

## RESPONSIBILITY FOR CARRYING OUT THE PROGRAM

When planning the homework center, it is imperative that the library assign responsibility for implementing and overseeing the new program. In other words, where will "homework help" appear on the library's organizational chart? Because the bulk of homework questions and after-school activities are handled by youth services staff, the coordination of formal homework assistance programs is often delegated to either the children's or teen services librarian. In large public libraries, like Los Angeles County, Chicago, and Cuyahoga County, the youth services coordinator typically oversees the library-wide program, while branch staff are responsible for the individual center's day-to-day operation. This arrangement provides a consistent homework help policy throughout the library, while encouraging flexibility at the local level. For example, at the Ventura County Library in California, branch staff are responsible for providing local service, even though the program as a whole is administered by the library's children's services manager.

Since most helpers tend to be volunteers, some homework programs are run out of the library's volunteer services department. In Sacramento, the Homework Zone is part of the library's overall volunteer program, which helps create a cohesive commitment to homework service, even though each site is tailored to its community's unique needs. Other libraries employ specialized staff to oversee their program. San Diego's Do Your Homework @ the Library program is funded completely through the mayor's office and so the head of the library's special projects division oversees the program. In King County, the Study Zone coordinator is a public services specialist. Homework help programs in Seattle and Prospect Heights, Illinois, are run by the library's school liaisons.

In a few libraries, homework help is actually outsourced to another organization. The Winters branch in Yolo County, California, offers an after-school program, called SUCCESS, in its community room two days a week. Although the library hosts the program, which is targeted at low-income migrant families, SUCCESS is completely managed by Rural Innovations in Social Economics, Incorporated (RISE, Inc.), a social services agency that receives funding from outside sources. A bilingual, full-time RISE employee not only supervises the operation, she is also very active in the community and so is an excellent conduit between parents and children who might need extra homework help. The Ventura County Library also outsources part of its systemwide homework centers. For many years, the Ojai Valley Library Foundation has funded and managed SchooLinks, an after-school homework program offered at every library branch in the Ojai Valley in California. In addition, two Ventura County branches host homework help through Project Understanding, a volunteer

**TALKING POINTS**

Though public libraries often include a promise to promote learning and education in their mission statements, they may not have a strategy for supporting students' homework needs. When developing a service plan for providing homework help, libraries should

- Develop specific goals and objectives to carry out the institution's educational mission. Not only do goals and objectives help define the services offered, they also create the standards against which those services will eventually be measured and evaluated.

- Carefully consider the level of homework help to be provided. Some programs are more intricate than others. What level of service is best for this library's community?

organization that provides free one-on-one tutoring to students who have been referred by local teachers.

## NOTES

1. Los Angeles Public Library, "About the Library," www.lapl.org/about-lapl/about-library.
2. Boston Public Library, "Mission Statement," www.bpl.org/general/trustees/mission.htm.
3. Hennepin County Library, "About the Library," www.hclib.org/about.
4. City of Santa Clarita Public Library, www.santa-clarita.com/city-hall/departments/public-library.
5. Saint Paul Public Library, "Mission and Vision," www.sppl.org/about/missionvision.
6. Los Angeles Public Library, "Student Zones," www.lapl.org/teens/homework-help/student-zones.
7. King County Library System, "Study Zone," kcls.org/study-zone/.

# STAFF AND VOLUNTEER RECRUITMENT

"MORE THAN ANYTHING, STAFF MAKES THE DIFFERENCE," EVA Mitnick, director of the Los Angeles Public Library's engagement and learning division, said about her institution's after-school Student Zone program (Jacobson 2016). Indeed, providing adequate staff is the single most important element in offering effective homework assistance. While some librarians call their curriculum-based collection of computers and reference materials a homework *center*, true homework *assistance* cannot happen without a staff member or volunteers to help students complete their work. Plus, many youngsters need the attention of an adult or peers to keep them on task when completing school assignments. They may also need validation to succeed.

The challenge, of course, comes in maintaining a paid or volunteer workforce that is large enough to provide sufficient assistance to the multitude of students who use the library every day after school. Most libraries cannot afford to hire the number of part-time employees needed to provide necessary homework help. Nor are they prepared to recruit and train a battery of after-school volunteers. Still, many libraries have succeeded in accomplishing this seemingly impossible task by maximizing the combined efforts of paid and volunteer staff.

## PAID VERSUS VOLUNTEER STAFF

Volunteers are a valuable asset to any homework assistance program. In fact, most homework centers would not exist without the help of trained volunteers. Paid employees are usually responsible for recruiting, training, and scheduling homework helpers, but it is often the volunteers themselves who provide the actual after-school assistance. At the Hennepin County Library in Minnesota, each homework help site has a team of three essential program personnel: a librarian, a paid lead tutor, and volunteers. More than 300 volunteers staff the program throughout the library.

In lieu of a salary, libraries give their volunteer homework helpers free parking passes, e-mail accounts, T-shirts, lapel pins, mugs, water bottles, and lots of recognition through public newsletters or special functions, such as volunteer teas or pizza parties. The motivation to volunteer can be extrinsic—for example, the chance to build one's résumé—or intrinsic. At the Lake City branch of the Seattle Public Library, a retired homework assistant said she enjoys helping kids because it's fun and the emotional reward is immediate. In addition, Seattle's 230 homework helpers have the opportunity to attend All-City Training on various topics, including teen behavior and race relations. Ninety percent of Seattle's homework helpers are adults.

Consistency is key in a program where young students expect to see familiar faces every day. Therefore, some libraries prefer to hire their homework helpers, rather than rely on the unpredictability of volunteers. The Boston Public Library, for instance, pays its teen "homework help mentors" $10 an hour and requires them to sign a contract stipulating that they will work the entire school year. Likewise, the Long Beach Public Library, in California, staffs its Family Learning Centers with paid learning guides, who work for the library year-round and help with the summer reading program. A similar arrangement exists at the County of Los Angeles Public Library, where homework helpers are permanent employees who work as shelvers during the summer.

In their joint "Homework Help Best Practices" statement, RUSA and YALSA recommend that an in-house staff person be designated to manage the homework center and train, coordinate, and schedule volunteers (YALSA Board of Directors Meeting 2015, 3). Brewer (1992) also recommends that a combination of paid and volunteer staff be used to operate the library's homework program. In Monterey County, part-time homework site coordinators are hired to oversee individual centers and recruit and schedule volunteer helpers. At the Castroville branch, for example, the site coordinator works closely with the local university to recruit "service learning" students, who are required to complete thirty hours of volunteer service per semester. The library gets free help from educated young adults, while the college students receive credit for required community service. Everybody wins!

## STAFF QUALIFICATIONS

Ludwig and Braun (2011b) argue that generalist public librarians cannot be expected to have the skills or knowledge necessary to assist with all school assignments. They therefore contend that if a library truly wants to make homework help a service priority, educators should be hired to work with kids after school. Many libraries, in fact, do look to local school districts for potential homework helpers who are either current or retired teachers. Perhaps the best example of this is the Chicago Public Library, where accredited teachers provide after-school homework help in most branch sites, four days a week. The educators, many of whom are bilingual, are paid through the privately funded Teacher in the Library program. Thousands of hours of assistance are provided library-wide every school year. In Boston, "teacher tutors" offer after-school homework help courtesy of the Boston Teachers Union. A schedule of the tutors' availability, which varies from branch to branch, is posted on the library's website.[1]

A newer, much smaller homework program is offered Thursday afternoons at the Dacula branch of the Gwinnett County Library, in Georgia. Here three volunteers—a retired teacher, a tutor with ten years' experience, and an adult education PhD—provide after-school assistance to local teens. Because of their strong educational background, the helpers required little training. Active as well as retired teachers are also integral to the success of homework programs in the Santa Maria Public Library's Los Alamos branch, as well as the Ellettsville branch of the Monroe County Library in Indiana.

Of course, not all homework helpers are teachers, nor should they necessarily be expected to have extensive educational backgrounds. Libraries should, however, appoint assistants who enjoy working with kids and are committed to helping them succeed in school. Previous experience working with youth, either in a paid or voluntary capacity, is often preferred. At the Winters branch in Yolo County in California, high school juniors and seniors become SUCCESS helpers only after spending one or two years as mentors-in-training. In Philadelphia, college-aged homework helpers become associate leaders in the library's LEAP program only after serving as teen leadership assistants during high school.

Other qualities are also highly desirable. The primary responsibility of the Los Angeles Public Library's homework helpers, for instance, is to assist students using Student Zone laptops to complete their school assignments. Therefore, strong knowledge of and experience with computers are mandatory. Homework helpers everywhere must also demonstrate good communication skills and, in at least one library, must be able to read aloud "expressively." The ability to read and speak in languages other than English is important, too. Across the country, libraries are being tasked with helping students who speak Spanish, Vietnamese, Farsi, Urdu, Japanese, Khmer, Korean, Russian, Tamil, Hindi, and Somali, among other languages. The coordinator of King County's Study Zone program maintains a list of bilingual homework helpers and exactly where and when they are scheduled each day, so students can be referred accordingly. Other more generic qualifications include problem-solving skills, patience, flexibility, organizational skills, ability to work as a team player, access to reliable transportation, and availability after school and on the weekend.

## RECRUITMENT

Homework assistants are generally recruited in the late summer and early fall, before the school year begins. Libraries use various methods of recruitment, including word of mouth, in-person conversations with community members, and printed flyers. A colorful brochure distributed by the Monterey County Free Libraries in California beckons prospective homework center volunteers by promising a "rewarding experience" where one can learn about library resources, explore science kits with students, and play educational games, in addition to helping children complete their homework.

Libraries also post recruitment announcements on their websites, linking either from the homework help site, general volunteer recruitment page, or from the library jobs page, if the position is paid. At the Bexley Public Library in Ohio, the online announcement for Homework Help Center Volunteer describes, in great detail, the purpose, responsibilities, requirements, and time commitment of the position.[2] In Hennepin County, the announcement for paid homework-help lead tutors includes program goals, the position's primary duties and responsibilities, minimum qualifications, number of hours per week, and hourly wage. (See appendix C for copies of staff recruitment announcements.)

Several libraries have made good use of established programs to provide homework assistants. These include Literacy Volunteers of America, AmeriCorps VISTA, Reserve Officers Training Corps, America Reads, Learning Is ForEver, and the Retired Senior Volunteer Program. YALSA and RUSA also recommend working with the National Honor Society to recruit teen homework volunteers. The Monroe County Library recruits potential helpers from a nearby naval base. In the past, librarians in San Diego County have teamed up with law enforcement officers to bring curriculum support and positive role models into the homework center. Not only did students get help with their assignments, but they also gained a new respect for the officers they may otherwise distrust.

College-aged helpers make good role models, too, especially in communities where dropout rates are high. In Minnesota, the Saint Paul Public Library recruits young adult assistants through local college work-study programs, which often pay up to 100 percent of the homework helper's salary. Education majors and members of the Future Teachers of America work especially well with younger kids. College students may even treat the homework center as a laboratory for testing their own teaching and disciplinary skills. At one library, the homework site coordinator used her daily experience as the basis for her master's thesis. At another, a homework assistant decided to become an education major as a direct result of working with kids every day.

Library staff also welcome the assistance of teenaged homework helpers. Despite occasional problems with teens forming cliques or flirting with each other, high schoolers perform as well as, if not better than, their older counterparts. At the La Habra branch of California's OC Public Libraries, sophomores, juniors, and seniors are recruited to help younger kids with their homework after school. Once they gain enough experience, they can ask to become a "tutor captain," who is

## TALKING POINTS

Providing adequate staff is the single most important element in offering an effective homework center. True homework assistance cannot happen without a staff member or volunteers to help students complete their assignments. When deciding which staffing configuration to employ, consider the following:

- Although in an ideal world all homework helpers would be paid for their efforts, in reality this isn't always possible. Therefore, experts agree that a combination of paid and volunteer staff should be used to carry out the library's homework program.

- While current and retired teachers may be preferred as homework helpers, noneducator volunteers also bring valuable knowledge and skills to the homework center. The best helpers are those who enjoy working with kids and are committed to seeing them succeed in school. Other qualifications may include knowledge of and experience with computers, ability to read and speak in languages other than English, problem-solving skills, patience, flexibility, and availability after school.

- Volunteers can be recruited from high schools, colleges, and community volunteer programs, and should be required to apply to become homework helpers. They should also be interviewed and, in most cases, undergo a thorough security check.

responsible for checking in and matching students with the appropriate helper. In our study of teen-assisted homework programs, Virginia Walter and I found that student helpers gain a sense of pride from serving their community, especially in low-income and ethnic neighborhoods, where they develop a keen sense of "giving back." We also learned that teen helpers are more socially competent and better prepared for the job market as a result of their homework center experience (Walter and Mediavilla 2003).

## THE HIRING PROCESS

Whether they are paid employees or volunteers, most prospective homework helpers undergo a process that requires completing an application form, passing an interview, and sometimes even taking an exam to test for certain competencies, such as math or English language proficiency. Applications may request information about prior work or volunteer experience, educational background, and the applicant's age or birthdate (see appendix D for sample application forms). The library may also want to know if the applicant has extensive knowledge of math or languages other than English. Prospective homework helpers should be ready to provide the names of one or two references as well as the name and phone number of an emergency contact. They may also be asked why they want to volunteer or become a homework helper and what times and days of the week they are available. At the Belle Cooledge branch of the Sacramento Public Library, teen helper candidates are required to submit a copy of their most recent report card and a written recommendation from at least one teacher. King County also requires a written recommendation from either a teacher or school counselor, verifying that the teen applicant has the maturity and skills required to work with peers.

Applicant qualifications may be further scrutinized via an interview, where candidates are asked to describe everything from their overall career goals to details about their past experiences working with children. Typical interview questions may include the following:

› Why do you think you would be an effective homework helper?
› What do you think is the most important benefit we offer students?
› A student you are working with gets upset and can't understand what you are trying to explain. Finally, the student tells you that you are not very good at explaining things at all. What would you say or do?
› How would you deal with children who don't want to be at the homework center, but whose parents insist they be there?
› What are some ways to motivate students to learn?
› In your past tutoring experience, have you ever had a situation where you could not help a student? What was the situation? What methods did you use to reach the student?
› What subjects do you have expertise in or are less familiar with? How would you help a student in those areas?

> › Tell us about your experience helping a student with a research project. How did you approach it? If you haven't helped a student with research, how did you approach your own project?
> › You may have several students needing help at the same time. How would you proceed? (Mediavilla 2001, 18)

After volunteer applicants pass the interview and agree to become part of the homework center staff, they then may be asked to sign a contract specifying duties and expectations (see appendix E for a sample contract). Generally, these contracts spell out a mutual working agreement and direct volunteers to immediately notify staff in case of absence. A parent or adult caretaker may also be asked to sign, if the homework helper is a minor. Finally, depending on the library, adult volunteers will probably undergo a security check and be fingerprinted.

## NOTES

1. Boston Teachers Union, "Need Help with Your Homework?" www.bpl.org/homework/BTU-Homework-Help-2016.pdf.
2. Bexley Public Library, Homework Help Center, "Homework Help Center Volunteer," bexleylibrary.org/sites/default/files/file/adult_volunteerdescription.pdf.

# JOB DUTIES AND TRAINING

TO DISTINGUISH THE DIFFERENT ROLES OF VARIOUS HOMEWORK CENTER staff, many libraries have developed job descriptions for both paid and volunteer workers (see appendix F for examples). These job descriptions not only identify the duties of homework helpers and site coordinators, they also describe what makes homework center staff distinct from other library employees.

For the most part, homework center staff are specifically hired and trained to work directly and exclusively with students. While other library staff may help kids by providing resources and reference services to answer academic questions, homework helpers take a more proactive role by advising students how to proceed with their schoolwork. Depending on the library's defined level of service, homework assistants may

› review class assignments
› explain instructions
› check student work
› drill youngsters in math and spelling
› help prepare for tests
› help strengthen children's reading skills

In other words, homework assistants ensure student success by providing the necessary tools and encouragement that enable young people to complete their schoolwork. As the Allen County Library tells its homework staff, "You're here to do what librarians are not able to do—help students understand and interpret their homework and help them learn the concepts necessary to complete the assignment" ("Instructions for Homework Helpers").

## JOB DUTIES

Homework center employees and volunteers may be called any one of a number of different titles. In Boston, teen helpers are called "mentors." At the Castroville branch of the Monterey County Free Libraries, the helpers are "service learners." Regardless of whether they are known as homework "tutors," "coaches," "buddies," "pals," or "assistants," their job duties generally range from helping students complete class assignments to keeping daily statistics. Tasks may include

> creating a neat and welcoming environment
> registering students and/or maintaining a daily log of homework center use
> setting up homework center materials, supplies, and equipment
> helping students complete homework assignments
> showing students how to use library resources
> developing supplementary learning materials
> helping students develop good study habits
> referring complicated research questions to the librarian
> troubleshooting problems related to using the library's computers
> serving as a mentor by listening to and talking with students about current issues and modeling positive values
> ensuring that students adhere to library rules of conduct
> acting as a liaison between the library and teachers to clarify assignments
> promoting the homework center through outreach and publicity
> assisting in the program evaluation process
> assisting staff in daily library operations (Mediavilla 2001, 20–21)

Other homework staff include supervisors who, in addition to helping students, may also run the program. Personnel at this level may be either paid or volunteer and are often called site or program "coordinators" or "lead" homework tutors or assistants. Their job duties tend to be more responsible and include tasks such as

> maintaining a generally positive learning atmosphere
> scheduling and training homework helpers
> helping students complete homework assignments
> matching students with appropriate homework helpers
> developing learning materials
> conducting regular staff meetings with homework helpers
> planning and presenting group programs for students and/or parents
> collaborating with library staff to carry out the goals of the program
> maintaining program records and submitting reports
> ordering supplies as needed
> working closely with parents and teachers to publicize the program and check on students' progress (Mediavilla 2001, 21)

## TRAINING

Before paid and volunteer staff can implement the tasks assigned, they need to be trained. It is no surprise, then, that the most effective after-school homework programs are those that make a priority of training new and continuing staff. In Monterey County, new helpers work at other branch homework centers for a week before starting at their regular site. They also participate in an orientation where they learn about the library's mission, its services, and automated circulation system. In King County, volunteer helpers are trained through an online orientation program that includes modules on

> job expectations and duties
> essential homework skills
> how to work with English-as-a-second-language learners
> addressing signs of child abuse
> parent and patron behavior
> conflict resolution (see appendix G for sample training modules)

Comprehension of King County's training content is tested via an online quiz administered by the program coordinator. Applicants must pass the quiz to work in the library's Study Zones.

In many cases, library staff conduct the helpers' orientation, which varies in length and depth depending on the structure and goals of the homework program. At the La Habra branch, teen homework help volunteers are required to attend a Saturday workshop, at the beginning of the school year, that is jointly led by the teen librarian and branch head. Snacks are provided. Topics covered include helper roles and responsibilities, homework help techniques, listening tips, student learning styles, and reading strategies. The emphasis is on teamwork and group problem-solving when challenges arise. Written exercises and role playing enliven the training session. The highlight, however, occurs at the end of the workshop when experienced peer helpers join the group to provide encouragement and firsthand advice to their rookie counterparts. "The best part of the job is seeing the look on kids' faces when they suddenly understand their homework," an older helper explains. Another advises not to take students' criticism personally. "Detach yourself and see where it goes," he says. At the end of the workshop, new and seasoned helpers sign up to work at least one day a week in the center.

## TALKING POINTS

Homework staff provide services that are often distinctly different from other library workers and volunteers. For this reason, it is imperative that their duties be explained in written job descriptions. They also need to be trained how best to carry out their tasks. Things to consider:

- While homework assistants generally help students complete class assignments, site supervisors may be responsible for scheduling and training homework helpers, matching students with appropriate homework helpers, developing learning materials, maintaining program records and submitting reports, and ordering supplies as needed.

- A library-led orientation should be mandatory for all homework help staff. At a minimum, this training should include an overview of the library's mission and the role of the homework center, a description of program policies, procedures, and performance expectations, copies of pertinent forms and schedules, an introduction to the library's resources and how to use them, techniques for working with students, an explanation of when questions should be referred to the librarian, and a tour of the facility.

Homework helpers are also trained by library staff and experienced volunteers at the Seattle Public Library. The two-hour orientation is held on a Saturday in September. The workshop agenda includes

> **Welcome and Overview** (15 minutes)
>   — Introductions of staff and new homework help volunteers
>   — Brief description of the program

> **Volunteer Panel: How We Assist Students** (15 minutes)
>   — Description of typical homework help sessions
>   — Helping students individually and in small groups
>   — Helping English-language learners
>   — How to handle students who are not familiar with the homework subject

> **Homework Help Scenarios** (30 minutes)
>   — Group exercise where volunteers discuss various homework help challenges and how to handle them

> **How Library Staff Can Help** (10 minutes)
>   — When to refer students to library staff
>   — Review of library resources, including materials for students researching college programs, scholarships, and preparing college applications

> **Homework Help Toolkit** (20 minutes)
>   — Review homework helper handbook

> **Volunteer Policies and Procedures** (5 minutes)
>   — Confidentiality and maintaining boundaries with students
>   — Tracking volunteer service hours
>   — Volunteer badges

> **Communication with Library Staff** (5 minutes)
>   — Staff contacts
>   — Reporting missed shifts

> **Concluding Remarks** ("Volunteer Orientation for Homework Helpers" 2015)

Regardless of who conducts the training, a well-organized homework center staff orientation should include a combination of the following:

> an overview of the library's mission and the role of the homework center
> a commitment to promoting a positive and safe learning environment
> a description of program policies, procedures, and performance expectations
> copies of pertinent forms and schedules

> an introduction to the library's resources and how to use them
> hands-on practice using library technology
> techniques for working with students
> an explanation of when questions should be referred to the librarian
> sensitivity to ethnic and cultural diversity
> a tour of the facility (Mediavilla 2001, 22–23)

Much of this information may also be presented as a handbook or manual that the homework staff can access in either a paper or online format. The Seattle Public Library, for instance, has an excellent "homework helper toolkit" that outlines performance expectations, homework help basics and resources, and ends with a school-year calendar. So, too, the Hennepin County Library provides a homework helper staff manual that includes a schedule and branch contact information, a description of the homework program and the helpers' role, resources and supplies, and performance expectations. (See appendix H for excerpted pages from sample staff manuals.)

In addition to written manuals and in-person orientation, some libraries also provide outside learning opportunities. Both the King County and Seattle public libraries encourage their homework assistants to attend free All-City Training workshops offered by school district trainers through the city of Seattle. In Boston, teen homework mentors undergo intensive supplemental training through Harvard University's Teaching and Learning Partnerships program. The training, called SmartTalk, emphasizes the dynamics that develop between mentors and students and how these can promote positive learning. Utilizing SmartTALK techniques, the teens become role models for the younger kids by helping them solve problems, by reading together with them every day, and by providing effective homework routines and support. The library, in turn, offers a place to learn and play in which youngsters feel safe, respected, and feel a sense of belonging (Moellman and Matsalia 2013). As the Harvard program's associate director Joan Matsalia explains, SmartTalk "realizes that success in school is about so much more than just finishing homework." With the library mentors' help, students "become more organized, develop better and stronger study skills, become more effective problem-solvers, and . . . work more effectively in groups" (O'Rourke 2014).

# FUNDING AND PARTNERSHIPS

A LTHOUGH SOME PROGRAMS, LIKE THOSE IN PASO ROBLES, CALIFORNIA, and the County of Los Angeles, are funded through the library's regular budget, most homework centers exist either solely, or in large part, thanks to outside funding sources. Occasionally, programs that began as grant-funded projects, such as LEAP in Philadelphia, become fully integrated into the library's service plan. For many, however, acquiring the resources to adequately staff and equip the center is an ongoing exercise that continually tests librarians' fund-raising and community-relations skills.

## FUNDING SOURCES

Over the years, library foundations have been extremely helpful in generating funds for after-school homework centers. Often acting as the program's fiscal agent, the library foundation can, as a nonprofit entity, apply for grants and other funding opportunities that are not usually made available to government agencies. The Library Foundation of Los Angeles, for instance, recently garnered a $1 million endowment from the Eli and Edythe Broad Foundation to support the Los Angeles Public Library's Student Zone program. The funds will buy updated laptops, tablets, printers, interactive whiteboards, and video cameras, plus pay for Student Zone helpers for more than half of the library's seventy-three branches (Jacobson 2016). In addition, the library's foundation continues to solicit donations from other funding agencies to support the Student Zone program.

Since the early 1990s, the Long Beach Public Library's Family Learning Centers have been completely supported through the fund-raising efforts of the library's foundation. Past donors include Bank of America, the *Los Angeles Times*, and Southern California Edison, all of whom are recognized through appropriate signage in the homework center space. Likewise, the Monterey County Free Libraries' multibranch homework program has flourished for many years thanks to the generosity of the library's foundation, which receives monies from the Community Foundation of Monterey County, the David and Lucile Packard Foundation, and the Monterey-based Harden Foundation. In Ventura County, the Ojai Valley Library Foundation has subsidized the library's SchooLinks program since 1996 through grants and donations from various local businesses and organizations.

Friends groups can also be a good source of financial support. In Hennepin County, the library's lead homework helpers are funded by the Friends of the Library. Meanwhile, back in Monterey County, the Friends of the Castroville Library sponsor extra hours for their homework center's site coordinator, so she can spend more time recruiting qualified homework helpers and work more closely with community members.

Individuals and private funders are also often generous sponsors of homework programs. The Alviso branch of the San José Public Library receives funds from the Legacy San José Alviso Youth Foundation, a local organization that specifically supports services to children in the rather isolated community of Alviso. Although branch staff must submit a grant application every year, the foundation remains supportive, providing funds for laptops, school supplies, incentive prizes, snacks, and a part-time homework helper. In Ventura County, homework assistance at the Prueter branch is funded by a private citizen, who loves his neighborhood library and believes in helping kids with their schoolwork. He pays for computer equipment, supplies, and sometimes even homework help staff.

Describing how to run a teen homework center on "minimum resources for most budgets," Brannon and Hildreth (2011) recommend approaching local businesses for possible funding. In particular, they suggest contacting Target, Walmart, and other national chains in order to identify their community-grant requirements. Area businesses are often happy to support educational programs at the library. Letters of intent, written to solicit support from private funders, should include

> a description of the program to be funded
> the target population
> the amount of money requested
> how the donation will be used

Brannon and Hildreth also recommend creating a separate budget, listing all items needed, in case the potential funder wants more details. (See appendix I for their sample letter of intent.)

When planning a homework center, YALSA and RUSA note that libraries may want to work with partner organizations in order to seek collaborative funding (YALSA Board of Directors Meeting 2015, 3). Using a "blended" model, Philadelphia's LEAP program receives support through private funds as well as from the state. Originally a Wallace Foundation "Public Libraries as Partners in Youth Development" grant project, LEAP is now part of PhillyBOOST, a network of agencies that provide out-of-school time (OST) services to young students. Partners in this effort are the city's human services department, which oversees programs for at-risk youth, and Philadelphia parks and recreation. PhillyBOOST not only funds the library's after-school program, it tracks young people's participation in OST activities across all three city departments, providing a snapshot of usage trends citywide. Funders include United Way, the William Penn Foundation, the Wallace Foundation, and the mayor's office.

## PARTNERSHIPS

Although not all homework programs require a lot of money, they do all require community commitment. Community partners not only help define the need for an after-school homework center, they also may support the program, either financially or through in-kind contributions, once it is launched. In fact, in many cases, public libraries can't sustain homework help without the generosity of partner organizations. Once library staff successfully identify and join forces with like-minded community agencies, a concerted effort to achieve academic success will soon follow.

In our book on outcome-based planning and evaluation, Melissa Gross, Virginia Walter, and I outline several strategies for making partnerships work. Chief among these is to look for partners that share a mission, purpose, and values similar to those of the library (Gross, Mediavilla, and Walter 2016, 48). Since 2006, the Brooklyn Public Library has partnered with 826NYC to offer an after-school homework and writing club, known as the Superhero Annex, in the basement of its Williamsburg branch. The project is part of the nationwide 826 initiative started by novelist Dave Eggers, who believes learning happens when kids receive one-on-one attention (Shaffer 2006). Volunteers provide after-school homework assistance four days a week in a space that evokes a superhero workroom. Not surprisingly, the program is so popular that prospective participants must register via a lottery. Students are required to bring and complete their homework before taking part in the center's other activities. The Boston Public Library's Grove Hall branch maintains a relationship with 826Boston, as well.

In Yolo County, the Winters branch library staff work with a social services agency, RISE, to offer after-school homework help three days a week. The target population is younger students, grades one through eight, who come from predominantly low-income and migrant families. The library provides space in its community room, while a RISE employee, funded through a three-year state grant, manages the program. Sharing a desire to enhance the local rural community's quality of life, the library and RISE collaborate to help young people become self-sufficient and succeed in school. A similar arrangement exists in Paso Robles, where a child-care agency and the library team up to offer after-school homework help to first through fifth graders. The Paso Robles Public Library operates its Library Study Center in a rent-free modular unit provided by the child-care partner. Other agencies in the facility's complex include First 5 California and the California State Preschool.

### TALKING POINTS

Although some libraries include the homework center as part of their regular budget, most programs exist thanks in part or largely due to outside funding. When seeking benefactors, libraries should look to

- Their own library foundations, which often act as fiscal agents to acquire outside gifts and grants. Friends groups, individuals, private funders, and local businesses have also generously supported library homework programs in the past.

- Like-minded community partners, especially those who initially helped identify the need for an after-school homework center. Once the program is launched, they may also want to support the program, either financially or through in-kind contributions.

Another important strategy for maintaining effective partnerships is to invite program staff to participate in the decision making. At the Los Angeles Public Library, Student Zone helpers are trained by the nonprofit organization Power-MyLearning, which emphasizes digital learning to improve educational outcomes. A major contributor to the success of the program, PowerMyLearning is a member of the project team that also includes the library's youth services coordinator and the Library Foundation of Los Angeles.

The Public Library Association has provided a thorough list of potential partners that should be involved in planning a homework center. These include

> the board of education
> home-school organizations
> the local chapter of the National Education Association
> parent-teacher organizations
> school personnel
> student councils
> teen centers (Garcia and Nelson 2007, 54)

In Boston and Monroe County, local teachers' unions pay their members to provide after-school homework assistance at the library. In Hennepin County, the library works with Generation Next, a local coalition that targets educational outcomes, to recruit qualified homework help volunteers. The Korean-American Parents Association, in Washington State, organizes and supervises teen homework helpers at the King County Library's Federal Way branch, and in Ventura County, the tutoring consortium Project Understanding provides free one-on-one homework assistance at the library's Foster and Saticoy branches. The Ventura group also donates school supplies and backpacks to participating students.

Community partners can also help support ancillary aspects of the library's homework program. The Lafayette Public Library in Colorado has an informal arrangement with the local middle school, which sends its residential bus by the library every day after school. Parents sign a permission slip if they want their children dropped off at the library's homework center. Their kids then pick up a special pass to ride the bus to the library that afternoon. The service is promoted on the library's homework center web page.[1] In Cuyahoga County, the Cleveland Food Bank makes food available at the library's homework centers. A healthy meal is also provided to youngsters for one hour during the homework program at the Lake City branch of the Seattle Public Library. The partner, in this case, is the Hunger Intervention Program, funded by the U.S. Department of Agriculture and offered through a local church.

**NOTE**

1. Lafayette Public Library, "Homework Center and Tutoring," cityoflafayette.com/1030/Homework-Tutoring.

# COLLABORATION WITH SCHOOLS

A LTHOUGH PUBLIC LIBRARIES AND SCHOOLS SHARE MANY OF THE SAME service goals, bringing the two entities together in a concerted educational effort is often a challenge. Librarians protest mass homework assignments that are impossible to handle with limited resources, while teachers complain that their local library is not adequately stocked with school-related materials. Homework centers may not resolve these particular issues, but if planned properly, they can provide a catalyst for school and library officials to begin working collaboratively together.

## TRADITIONAL COMMUNICATION

Librarians and educators agree that one of the main barriers to successful homework completion is the lack of communication between local schools and the public library. Kids suffer when the library doesn't receive advance notice of homework assignments or when school officials are unaware of library hours and regulations. Librarians, therefore, have developed several tried-and-true methods of communicating with their local schools. In Monterey County, library staff send a letter to teachers at the beginning of the school year to promote the branches' homework help services. In other libraries, like King County, homework helpers send a letter to the teacher advising when an assignment is too difficult for the student to complete. (See appendix J for sample teacher letters.)

Perhaps the most common method of communication is the "homework alert" form, which is posted on many public library websites. As its name implies, the purpose of the form is to alert library staff to upcoming assignments, so they can prepare accordingly. Some libraries temporarily reserve pertinent materials for "library use only" during the duration of a big assignment, or they may limit how many items a student can check out on a particular homework topic. Intner (2011) recommends that the homework alert form be as succinct as possible, so teachers will actually complete and submit it. Important information for teachers to provide includes

> school name
> library branch(es) students might use to complete the assignment
> teacher's name and contact information (e-mail is preferable)
> grade level
> course title/subject area
> number of students or classes working on the assignment
> start and due dates
> required materials (e.g., particular titles, formats, etc.)
> excluded materials (e.g., particular formats)
> description of the assignment
> box to check if the assignment is annual
> teacher's request to reserve materials for students to use in the library
> teacher's request to receive a bibliography or other materials relevant to the assignment
> other relevant information (Intner 2011, 37–38)

Some librarians have compiled lists of "homework tips" to make library visits as productive as possible for students and teachers alike. These lists provide helpful homework hints to students, while encouraging teachers to carefully plan their research assignments. At the Queens Public Library, in New York, students are advised to

> bring their own supplies, including homework assignments, paper and pencils, money for the photocopier, textbooks, and library cards
> maximize use of the library's print and electronic resources
> sign up early to use the library's computers
> ask the librarian for suggestions on how to use library resources
> never cut pictures out of library books or magazines[1]

As for teachers, library staff suggest that they

> assign a choice of reading options, rather than a single title for every student to read
> avoid "mass assignments" on the same subject
> notify librarians of homework assignments in advance
> visit the library to make sure it owns the materials required to complete the assignment
> accept references from a variety of print and electronic resources
> provide opportunities for students to do research in the school library
> give assignments in writing, rather than verbally, to eliminate confusion and misinterpretation
> stagger major research projects and allow enough time to complete them
> encourage the use of student-generated illustrations, rather than pictures from magazines or books
> remind students that librarians can relay only brief information over the phone (Mediavilla 2001, 30)

## WORKING TOGETHER

As efficient as lists, forms, and letters might be, sometimes the best communication occurs when school officials and librarians work together directly to achieve their educational goals. "We need to begin the conversation," *Knowledge Quest* blogger Kate MacMillan (2017) insists, acknowledging the rift that often exists between schools and public libraries. "Yes, we have different roles, but in the long run we are here to provide the best services we can."

In Monroe County, twenty years of monthly meetings, between local school librarians and public library staff, ultimately resulted in the teachers' union agreeing to pay the salary of a lead homework tutor, who provides after-school math assistance to teens at the library. At the Los Alamos branch in Santa Maria, California, the site coordinator often meets with the nearby school's "bilingual liaison," who then reminds parents which days and times their children are scheduled for after-school homework help.

Spontaneous one-on-one communication can also be effective. The coordinator of King County's Study Zones tells of an eight-year-old Iraqi student who was struggling with math and so came to the library for assistance. When the homework helper discovered that the student wasn't allowed to take her textbook  home, the coordinator contacted the school librarian, who then e-mailed the child's teacher. Within twenty-four hours, the homework helper received a copy of the textbook, which was then used to assist the student. Study Zone helpers are also empowered to refer more challenging situations back to the school district, which provides free tutoring to students who qualify for the service.

Some public libraries have designated staff, whose job is to work closely with schools and students. The library's youth services school liaison in Prospect Heights, Illinois, regularly attends school events and staff meetings to promote the homework center as well as recruit teenaged "study buddies" (Prospect Heights Public Library District 2014). In Seattle, the formal learning librarian, who also manages the library's homework help program, is responsible for interacting with the school district. When community members approach the library about starting a homework center in their local branch, she confers with school officials to decide just how necessary such a service might be. Though the Palos Verdes Library District, in California, no longer offers formal after-school homework help, they do have a full-time school and student services librarian who networks with school administrators and introduces library resources to both students and teachers. A recent workshop, aimed at high schoolers, taught teens how to detect fake news.

The Nashville Public Library recently teamed up with the Metro Nashville Public Schools to maximize use of the library's

### TALKING POINTS

Bridging the rift that often divides public libraries and schools can be a challenge. Nevertheless, some public libraries have found innovative ways to effectively collaborate with their school partners by

- Designating a staff liaison, who regularly meets and communicates with teachers and other school officials. In Seattle, for instance, new homework centers are created only after conferring with the school district.

- Making their resources directly available to students through the local schools. Both Nashville and the three public library jurisdictions in New York City are successfully circulating materials that are regularly delivered to school districts. In Nashville, the program has resulted in improved reading skills, higher grades, school retention, higher test scores, and improved English-language achievement. Student use of the public library has also increased.

collection. Called Limitless Libraries, the program gives more than 25,000 students, grades three through twelve, access to public library materials that are delivered to their schools by daily courier. Students use their unique school identification number to request and check out materials. More than 112,000 items were circulated in 2013, including books, audiovisual materials, e-books, netbooks, Nooks, and iPad minis, as well as materials for English-language learners. Project evaluators found a direct correlation between students' participation in Limitless Libraries and improved reading skills, higher grades, school retention, higher test scores, and improved English-language achievement. Student use of the public library also increased as a result of the program (Lance, Schwarz, and Rodney 2014).

The Brooklyn, Queens, and New York public libraries offer a similar service in partnership with the New York City Department of Education. Called MyLibraryNYC, the collaboration provides vetted sets of books to some 550 schools that have libraries staffed by credentialed librarians. Book sets include topics, such as "LGBTQ Fiction and Nonfiction" (grades preschool through third), "Fighting for a Cause: Civil Rights Picture Books" (grades second through third), "Native Americans in New York" (grades four through five), and "Great Books for 11th & 12th Grade!" as well as multiple copies of books by Lois Lowry, Maya Angelou, David McCullough, and Toni Morrison. In addition, an array of professional development resources is made available to educators. Teachers and students can also access the electronic databases of all three public libraries from school or home. During the 2014/15 academic year, more than 300,000 items were circulated from the Brooklyn Public Library alone through MyLibraryNYC (Barack 2015; Callaci 2015). Although not strictly related to after-school homework centers, the success of both this and the Nashville program illustrates how public libraries and schools can work together to positively impact student performance.

---

## NOTE

1. Queens Library, "Homework Help and Hints," www.queenslibrary.org/Kids/homework-help/homework-help-and-hints.

# SPACE AND LOCATION

WHETHER THE PROGRAM IS OFFERED IN AN ISOLATED ROOM OR IS fully integrated into the library's overall floor plan, a dedicated area to meet students' after-school needs is essential to the definition of a homework center. Not only does the space itself distinguish a *center* from other types of homework service, such as online tutoring or virtual websites, but it also gives kids a sense of place where they can make homework a priority. Moreover, physical boundaries enable staff to control and constructively focus the energies of students as they participate in the program. Since quiet and studious behaviors are required to complete one's schoolwork, the library's rules of conduct are usually more enforceable within the perimeters of the homework center.

According to Ludwig and Braun (2011b), the first requirement for a successful homework help program is "space for [kids] to use resources . . . and collaborate." After all, students need room where they can talk and work together, spread out, brainstorm on how to complete an assignment, and even eat and drink, if allowed. Ludwig and Braun further contend that public libraries offer the best learning environment because they provide up-to-date technology and are free of the distractions of home. RUSA and YALSA concur, admonishing libraries to "designate a space where homework help/tutoring is the primary service, and where all associated materials and equipment, if any, are assembled" (YALSA Board of Directors Meeting 2015, 3). The Public Library Association is even more specific, recommending that libraries, hoping to help students succeed in school, make available

> › space for a homework center
> › study rooms or other space for students to work
> › workstations that are large enough to allow several students to work together
> › ergonomic furniture (Garcia and Nelson 2007, 56)

Still, finding room for even a part-time homework program can be difficult in an already crowded facility. The homework center can be noisy and often has to compete with other after-school programs held in the same small area at the same time. At one site, homework help ended up displacing the library's literacy program, which was previously located in a secluded part of the stacks. Despite these obstacles, library staff have found practical yet creative ways to accommodate the space needed to provide after-school homework assistance.


## SEPARATE SPACES

To minimize noise that might disrupt other users after school, many homework programs are held in library meeting rooms or other enclosed spaces located away from the public. Staff and parents alike appreciate having homework activity closely supervised within the confines of the room, while students enjoy the freedom to chat among themselves and with helpers. Participants may even be allowed to eat and drink while studying in a secluded part of the building. Also, when the room is separate from the rest of the library, business hours are easier to schedule because the space is closed during school hours. Jurisdictions that conduct homework help in their community rooms include the Monterey County Free Libraries, Cuyahoga County Public Library, Sacramento Public Library, the Winters branch in Yolo County, and Orange County's La Habra branch.

Some libraries provide off-site homework help. For many years, the Monterey Public Library offered its Homework Pals program through a local elementary school. The library recruited, trained, scheduled, and supervised a battery of volunteers who then provided homework help at the school. Although the library ran the program, the school assumed responsibility for all security matters. In the early 1990s, the Orange Public Library ran the Friendly Stop, a stand-alone homework center that was open weekday afternoons for three hours. The facility, a modular unit owned by the school district, sat in a park in the middle of a Latino barrio. Children stopped by and got homework help on their way home from school.

Perhaps the best example of an off-site homework help program today is the Library Study Center in Paso Robles, California. Originally started as a corollary service to an after-school arts program in 1999, the Library Study Center moved to its current site in 2010. Located across the street from low-income housing and a dual-language-immersion elementary school, the center is part of a complex that includes First 5 California, a state-supported program for young children, and the California State Preschool. The library's program targets students, kindergarten through fifth grade, and primarily serves youngsters from the immediate neighborhood. The facility is a former modular classroom, furnished with tables, chairs, and cozy sofas and decorated in colorful murals. A sign asks students to deposit their backpacks by the door, either on hooks or on the floor. The entire room is kid-friendly and warm. Homework help is provided by library staff and volunteers for two hours, Monday through Thursday, during the school year. In the summer, the space is open four days a week for two hours, following the school district's free lunch program.

As preferable as remote sites may be, there are distinct disadvantages to these types of homework centers. Unlike programs provided in the library's more visible areas, isolated centers must, for security reasons, be constantly staffed with on-site personnel. This, in turn, may seriously curtail how frequently homework help is offered, particularly in libraries with limited staff. In addition, site-specific homework programs often have to compete with other activities occupying the same space. At a branch in Sacramento, for instance, the homework center, open just one afternoon a week, shares the community room with a weekly coding program and in-library job center. Maintaining remote programs is even more tenuous when homework assistance is offered off-site. In Orange, the program faced extinction when the school district decided it had more lucrative uses for the building that housed the Friendly Stop. Luckily, the community rallied in favor of retaining the program and so the lease was extended another two years. But sustaining programs in borrowed space can be a challenge, especially when that square footage could otherwise be used to generate revenue through room rental or other fees.

Another important issue is that remote homework centers usually lack a "library context." Providing programs in community rooms, schools, or partner-owned facilities may be efficient, but they rarely help cultivate strong library study habits. Also, some redundant services, like photocopying, may need to be added if the homework center is too far removed from the rest of the library. Computer equipment and a duplicate homework-related collection may also have to be provided.

## INTEGRATED FLOOR PLANS

When no meeting room or other secluded space is available, homework assistance ends up being offered on the library's open floor. At the Lake City branch in Seattle, for example, five tables in the center of the library are turned into a homework center four days a week. A sign, indicating that "Homework Help Is in Session," lets everyone know that the space is now designated for students and their helpers. In smaller outlets, like the Castroville branch in Monterey County, the entire building becomes a hub of after-school activity, with homework help the top priority for both staff and students.

Despite possible noise and other control issues, most librarians report positive results from unrestricted, open-area homework centers. Comfortably surrounded by resources and peers, kids begin to think of the library as a "place of their own" and may even return during non-school days. Homework areas need not be large, but they should always be clearly defined so studious behaviors can be enforced. Though corner spaces help identify the area as something unique and special, homework centers should always be clearly visible from public service desks. The look and location of the program should also reflect the age group being targeted. Teenagers, for instance, will resist any suggestion that they study in the children's room. Intner (2011) recommends that staff work with the library's teen advisory board to design homework-friendly areas that appeal to adolescents (35–36). In Brossard, Quebec, staff consulted with local teens before converting the library's basement into a young adult space. Since one of their goals was to facilitate school success, more than 50 percent of the square footage is allocated to after-school workspace for teenaged students (Brisson 2014).

One of the most effective homework environments is The Quad, a branded micro-space that makes the Los Angeles Public Library's Student Zones immediately recognizable. Erected on the floor of twenty branches, the large blue structures feature a powered laptop bar and desk as well as soft seating for more relaxed study. Each Student Zone site also provides access to laptops, free school supplies, and a homework helper. "Homework is not always about writing a term paper, but it's also about collaborating with your friends or snuggling up to read a good book," The Quad's designer Cort Grosser says. "The Quad facilitates all of this and leverages design for a greater educational good."[1] Indeed, the space makes after-school homework help feel like an exclusive club and yet is clearly visible from the reference desk. Year-end statistics for 2015/16 show a 57 percent increase in Student Zone use since The Quads were installed, with repeat use tripling (Library Foundation of Los Angeles 2016). Needless to say, The Quads are extremely popular and always abuzz with homework activity after school.

---

**NOTE**

1. Cort Grosser & Associates, "Student Zones_LA Public Library," www.corygrosser.com/Student-Zones-_-La-Public-Library.

# SERVICE HOURS

RUSA AND YALSA RECOMMEND THAT PUBLIC LIBRARIES SET SPECIFIC hours for in-person homework help during out-of-school time (YALSA Board of Directors Meeting 2015, 3). Indeed, younger students, in particular, rely on consistency and so are more likely to use the library's homework center if its hours of operation are predictable as well as plentiful. Unfortunately, however, many homework-assistance schedules seem more driven by limited library resources than by student need. The fewer staff who are available to oversee the program, the fewer hours the homework center is open. Out of necessity, the library's homework help service is often restricted to the resources at hand.

## SCHEDULING FACTORS

Although it may seem obvious that *after-school* programs occur between the hours of 2:30 and 6:00 PM, several factors must first be considered when scheduling homework help. Programs for younger students tend to be offered right after school when parents and other caregivers are working. The Boston Public Library, for instance, provides homework help from 3:30 to 5:30 PM, Monday through Thursday, at twenty-one branches. The Los Angeles Public Library's Student Zones are offered Monday through Thursday, from 2:30 to 6:00 PM. If managing unattended children is a chronic issue, staff may decide to stagger homework help days to preclude an unwanted day-care situation. At the now-defunct program in San Leandro, California, students were allowed to sign up for homework assistance on Monday and Wednesday or Tuesday and Thursday, but not all four days. On the alternate days, kids were encouraged to visit day-care facilities elsewhere so the library would not become the only after-school option for unattended youth.

Unlike younger students, few teens have time to do homework right after school. Therefore, programs for high school students should be scheduled later in the day or even on the weekend. In Fort Wayne, Indiana, homework assistance is offered from

6:00 to 8:00 PM, Monday through Wednesday, in the library's teen department. In San Diego, weekday homework help hours are extended to Friday through Sunday at the central library, since those days tend to attract older students.

Occasionally libraries will offer separate programs for children and older kids. The Lafayette Public Library in Colorado, for example, provides general homework assistance to all ages, 2:45 to 6:30 PM, Monday through Thursday, but restricts advanced math and physics help to high school students only. While the math/physics program is held from 5:00 to 6:30 PM in a room upstairs, the more general program is offered downstairs. The advanced program is scheduled later in the day to accommodate both the volunteers and high schoolers' busy lives.[1] Separate homework programs are also offered in Mission Viejo, California, where advanced math assistance is provided to students, grades seven through twelve, in the evening, while general homework help is provided to students, grades two through six, in the afternoon. Both programs are filled to capacity.[2]

Some libraries also stagger the days and times of their programs to maximize the use of their branch facilities. Space is so limited at the Sacramento Public Library that its Homework Zone program is offered only one day a week at most branches. To provide as broad coverage as possible, staff try not to schedule their weekly session at the same day or time as nearby branches. This way, students can conceivably travel from branch to branch as needed during the week. Likewise, in Monroe County, math help is offered at the central library, Monday evenings, and at the Ellettsville branch on Wednesday. Several of the same students make use of both sites.

Staff must also consider that not all youngsters have ready access to transportation. If the homework center is located in a remote or notoriously dangerous part of town, services should be scheduled early enough to allow kids to walk home safely during daylight. At the Friendly Stop in Orange, children always left before dark. Therefore, business hours were regularly changed according to the season to accommodate early and late sunsets.

Although in many jurisdictions it's the busiest day of the week, most libraries have canceled Saturday homework help sessions due to lack of interest. Sunday programs, on the other hand, can be extremely popular, possibly because assignments are due on Monday. In Saint Paul, Minnesota, students respond well to Sunday assistance because the library tends to be less crowded, allowing more one-on-one time with the homework helper. The Family Learning Centers in Long Beach, California, are also far better used on Sunday than on Saturday.

## TALKING POINTS

More students will use the homework center if its hours of operation are both predictable and plentiful. The County of Los Angeles Public Library recommends considering community priorities when scheduling homework programs. At what time do schools let out? When do kids have access to the library? On which days do school holidays usually occur? Other considerations include

- Teens and homework volunteers' busy lives. What are the best times to attract older kids and adult helpers?

- Stretching limited resources. Can branches stagger their homework help schedules so nearby programs aren't offered on the same days and times?

- Special school-related circumstances. For instance, can the library extend its hours during finals week?

## FINALS WEEK

Ludwig and Braun (2011b) argue that libraries should do whatever they can to support homework completion during the days and hours when students need the most help. In particular, they urge administrators to extend hours during high school finals week. There is little need for extra staffing during these times, they insist, because "teens cramming for tests are usually fairly self-sufficient."

In 2007 the Hinsdale Public Library, in Illinois, held its first "Finals Service" program after staff began noticing a huge influx of teenagers at the end of the school year. To address the situation, the librarians decided to offer as much library space as possible to high school students studying for their final exams. Space was made available in the library's community room, storytime area, study rooms, all "nooks and crannies," and even on the outside patio. Although one community member complained about the newspaper area being full of teens, staff were pleased at how comfortable the students seemed using the library. Over 300 people participated in the program in its first year (Elam, Auxier, and Boland 2009).

More recently, the Carrollton Public Library has begun offering a program, called "Let's Get Crammin,'" at the end of every semester. Because the library's meeting rooms are quickly booked, special tables are set up for group study in the conference room. School supplies and snacks are provided, but no homework helpers are needed because the students themselves solve the assigned test problems within their own groups.[3] The Arlington Public Library in Virginia runs a similar program, called "After Hours Study Night." Held on the Sunday before exams begin, the library remains open from 9:00 until 11:00 PM for high school students only. Several teachers voluntarily sign up to lead the study groups, while the library provides pizza, snacks, and coffee, all paid for by the local parent-teacher association. In 2015 over 250 people participated in the program.[4]

## SUMMER AND HOLIDAYS

Even if school is not offered during the summer, some libraries continue to operate their homework programs year-round. During June and July, the homework center may be transformed into the library's summer reading club or the site of other noncurricular educational activities. In Paso Robles, the Library Study Center is open four days a week for two hours, following the school district's free lunch program. Homework help at the San Diego Public Library (SDPL) also remains active during the summer, from 3:00 to 6:00 PM, Monday through Thursday, at nine branches and the central library. The SDPL also offers free summer learning camps through the Do Your Homework @ the Library program.

Winter can wreak havoc on homework schedules, especially in regions where schools are regularly closed for "snow days" or other weather-related complications. And then, of course, there are the holidays and winter break, when schools nationwide are closed for at least two weeks. RUSA and YALSA advise libraries to clearly post homework center times, cancellations, and scheduled holidays so students can plan accordingly (YALSA Board of Directors Meeting 2015, 3).

**NOTES**

1. Lafayette Public Library, "Homework Center," www.cityoflafayette.com/1030/Homework -Tutoring.
2. Mission Viejo Library, "Homework Help & Tutoring," cityofmissionviejo.org/departments/ library/library-services/homework-help-tutoring.
3. James Celadon, YA-YAAC e-list conversation on April 5, 2016, archived at lists.ala.org/sympa/ arc/ya-yaac.
4. Lisa Cosgrove-Davies, YA-YAAC e-list conversation on April 6, 2016, archived at lists.ala.org/ sympa/arc/ya-yaac.

# PROGRAMMING AND COROLLARY SERVICES

**10**

WHILE MOST PUBLIC LIBRARIES PROVIDE BASIC HOMEWORK ASSIS-
tance after school, a few exceed expectations by offering
ancillary services that help students enhance their scholastic
experience and build skills. In Yolo County and Philadelphia,
homework help is part of a larger, more intrinsic enrichment
program. Other jurisdictions provide immediate, more extrin-
sic rewards by offering tangible incentives, such as raffles and educational games, to
motivate kids to complete their homework. Regardless of how they are configured,
supplemental programming and other corollary services represent the library's
sincere desire to best support students' learning needs.

## ENHANCED HOMEWORK HELP

For some libraries, helping kids succeed in school means more than just offering
homework assistance. At the Seattle Public Library, for instance, four branches provide high school mentors, called "learning buddies," to read and play math games
with elementary school-aged English language learners. This first-come-first-served
program is offered once a week for an hour and is drop-in only. In 2017, 64 percent
of youngsters said their attitude toward reading and math improved as a result of
participating in the program, while 54 percent reported actually improving their
math and reading skills (Seattle Public Library 2017).

In Brooklyn, elementary, middle, and high school students can reserve a reference librarian, for half an hour, to help research a homework project. Appointments
are made via an online form that asks the student to describe the school assignment
in detail. The librarian then contacts the student, either by phone or e-mail, and
sets a time for both of them to meet at the central library over the next week. The
"Book-a-Librarian" program is available to registered cardholders only.[1]

The Brooklyn Public Library's Williamsburg branch also partners with 826NYC,
a nonprofit organization dedicated to supporting the educational needs of students

from ages six through eighteen. The program is available in the tutoring annex four afternoons a week. Designed as a superhero headquarters, the tutoring annex is so popular that young people must apply months in advance to participate. Preference is given to applicants whose families are economically disadvantaged. Once their homework is completed, the kids are given creative writing assignments to work on with staff and volunteer homework helpers. The best writing samples are then collected and published as an "826NYC Review" anthology at the end of the school year.[2]

Another tactic for improving students' homework experience is to train their parents how to better help with school assignments. In 2014 the Santa Clarita Library in California conducted "Homework Help, Parent Edition," a three-part workshop designed to provide Spanish-speaking parents with the skills and knowledge needed to help their children complete schoolwork at home. By the end of the series, 58 percent of parents read to their children three or more times a week, 79 percent assisted with homework three or more times a week, and 95 percent had checked their child's schoolwork three or more times a week (City of Santa Clarita Public Library 2015, 5).

## ENRICHMENT PROGRAMS

For some libraries, the homework help program is only part of an overall strategy to enrich the lives of young people. In Yolo County, RISE, Inc. offers the after-school program SUCCESS at the Winters library, three days a week. Aimed at first through eighth graders, SUCCESS was started in 2009 to respond to the community's urgent request for homework help programs. Children are enrolled for the entire year, including summer, and are mentored by high school students. Though academic achievement is a priority, only half the time is actually spent doing schoolwork. The rest of the time, youngsters read or complete educational worksheets provided by the program coordinator. In addition, either branch staff or the local high school librarian provides a weekly book talk to further engage the kids in reading. The branch librarian also conducts a monthly Community World Café discussion with all the mentors and younger students together. A recent session on immigration elicited critical expression through art and poetry. The goal here is to create a socially supportive environment where participants can acquire the skills needed to succeed academically as well as emotionally. To measure achievement, a "happiness questionnaire" and mental health survey are administered to each child several times a year. Included on the survey are questions about personal and academic achievements.

In 2013, the New York Public Library (NYPL) launched a series of after-school programs that incorporate a strong homework help component. Enrichment Zones, for students in grades one through eight, are offered in ten branches two to four days a week. Among the services provided are daily homework support; developing Common Core State Standards reading and math skills; educational computer games; and hands-on science, math, and writing activities.[3] Three other branches offer Innovation Labs, where middle school students work together to address community issues via podcasts, blogs, and video game design. The purpose is to help young people develop the problem-solving and critical-thinking skills required by Common Core, while also supporting homework completion.[4] Then there is BridgeUP, a five-year program that offers long-term mentoring and educational support to a select group of adolescents, starting in eighth grade and continuing until high school graduation. As part of the BridgeUP experience, student "scholars" are invited to participate in field trips and other special events. Potential candidates must apply and be interviewed before being accepted into the program.[5]

Perhaps the best-known and certainly longest-lived youth enrichment program is LEAP, started by the Free Library of Philadelphia in 1990. Formerly the Literacy Enrichment Afterschool Program, LEAP initially began as an educational and cultural program to help manage overwhelming after-school use by kids. Today the emphasis is on offering out-of-school time services in general, with a main emphasis on STEAM programming and creating a shared club-like atmosphere. Although the program appeals primarily to African American and Hispanic youth, all students, kindergarten through twelfth grade, are welcome. The library employs "teen leadership assistants" and college-aged "associate leaders," who not only provide mentoring and homework help at the branches, but also serve as role models in communities that often lack positive examples for young people to emulate (Walter 2009). LEAP activities promote traditional learning as well as literacy in science, technology, and the cultural arts.

## COROLLARY ASSISTANCE

During the Great Recession that began in 2008, public libraries were inundated with unemployed community members and others seeking career advice. To meet this demand, the Columbus Metropolitan Library in Ohio converted its homework centers into job centers for most of the day, except for the three hours directly after school when students used the facilities. Library staff, volunteers, and partner agencies, such as the Urban League and Family Services, helped people search for jobs and hone their workplace skills ("Homework Help Converted to Job Help Centers" 2009).

A similar program continues in Long Beach, California, where the library's larger Family Learning Centers remain open all day. The space, which is filled with computers usually reserved for kids doing homework, has become an informal career center where users of all ages can get job and résumé help during the morning and evenings. Some of the Family Learning Centers also have 3-D printers, which can be used for projects not necessarily related to homework assignments.

At some libraries, helping students complete college applications or apply for financial aid is considered a natural extension of the homework center's educational mission. Homework helpers in King County are allowed to help students complete college and scholarship applications. Likewise, homework volunteers in Hennepin County are welcome to help teens apply for college, scholarships, and even job openings, but are encouraged to follow up with library staff, who might be able to find further resources for the students to use (Hennepin County Library 2016a).

## INCENTIVES

Because it is often difficult to motivate young children, in particular, to do their homework, some libraries have devised incentive programs to reward positive learning behavior. At the La Habra library, students can earn up to five stars a day if they complete all their school assignments and demonstrate a positive attitude. They can also earn two extra stars if they read for at least ten minutes. After twenty stars, the student, accompanied by the homework helper, can pick an item from the homework center's prize box. To minimize disputes, the helpers are required to track all stars and rewards.

In Paso Robles, the Library Study Center coordinator makes note of homework activity and gives each child a round token as a reward. Once a week, the kids can exchange their tokens for a piece of candy, school supplies, or a trip to the "treasure box." Although most youngsters turn in two tokens right away for candy, some are more patient and so are rewarded with bigger and better prizes. The exercise not only recognizes the kids for doing their homework, it also teaches responsibility and the benefits of being patient.

Good study behaviors are also rewarded in King County, where helpers are encouraged to give stickers to students who complete especially challenging homework assignments or are facing a difficult test the next day. "It doesn't have to be an 'A' or a perfect score to be a major accomplishment," the Study Zone staff manual admonishes. "Praise any improvement that a student worked hard for." But additional gifts beyond the stickers are verboten. After all, as the manual reminds the helpers, "Your time is your greatest gift!"

## NOTES

1. Brooklyn Public Library, "Book a Librarian Appointment Request," bpl.brooklynpublic library.org/bal.
2. 826NYC, "After-School," 826nyc.org/program/afterschool/.
3. New York Public Library, "Enrichment Zones," www.nypl.org/ost/enrichmentzone.
4. New York Public Library, "Middle School Innovation Labs," www.nypl.org/ost/middle -school-labs.
5. New York Public Library, "BridgeUP," www.nypl.org/ost/bridgeup.

# LIBRARY RESOURCES

**I**N COMMUNITIES THAT OFFER SEVERAL AFTER-SCHOOL HOMEWORK ASSISTANCE options, a collection of books and online resources often distinguishes the public library's homework center from all the rest. Providing written materials to support students' academic needs is, after all, one of the things libraries have always done well. It is no surprise, then, that RUSA and YALSA recommend the following "best practices" when assembling a homework-related collection:

> › Rebrand existent collections and subscriptions to provide obvious links to homework services.
> › Establish a reference collection specifically for in-house use by students and homework helpers.
> › Contact school representatives or the school librarian to ensure that the library's holdings support course assignments and the curriculum.
> › Develop an online collection of resources by subject.
> › Offer online tutoring services (YALSA Board of Directors Meeting 2015, 3).

Many successful public library homework centers already incorporate these practices.

## COLLECTION DEVELOPMENT CONSIDERATIONS

Although online resources may now attract more attention than books, many librarians still equate a strong curriculum-based print collection with effective homework help. Depending on the library, the homework center's collection may consist of a cart filled with a handful of ready-reference titles, or it may be a distinctly designated part of the youth services or teen section. The size and placement of the homework center's collection should reflect not only student needs, but also the extent to which the items duplicate or complement nearby school libraries. Before the collection is created, staff should determine whether students require

## TALKING POINTS

Books and online resources often help distinguish the library's homework center from other after-school programs in the community. Still, in many cases, these materials are superfluous to school assignments that rely more heavily on teacher-generated worksheets. When building a collection that supports homework assistance, be sure to consider the following:

- Instead of buying all new materials, review the library's existing collection to see what titles might be repurposed for homework help. Encyclopedias, dictionaries, writing manuals, and other reference-type materials can be "borrowed" and reshelved near the homework center.

- Although books may seem to be losing favor to higher-demand online sources, the Common Core State Standards still emphasize the printed word. Therefore, historic works, as well as established "classics" and contemporary titles of literary merit, should be retained and featured as part of text sets that help students compare and contrast topics.

- Links to authoritative websites and subscription databases should be featured via a curated web page that lists homework-related resources. The Multnomah County Library's virtual "Homework Center" is an excellent example of an online tool that is immensely informative as well as attractive.

- Online tutoring services are not only a godsend for students who are stumped by that day's homework assignment, they are also appreciated by staff. Especially appealing is the fact that virtual homework help is anonymous, thus minimizing the pressure for youngsters to perform well.

supplemental materials to complete their homework or if assignments are based strictly on textbooks and worksheets. Also, are reference materials necessary to meet mass assignment demands, or is the circulating collection adequate? Finally, what formats are kids required to use, especially in light of Common Core?

When establishing a homework assistance collection, staff may want to pull—and "rebrand," as RUSA and YALSA suggest—items from other parts of the library to expedite the development process. Brannon and Hildreth (2011) warn against including books with the words "dummy" or "idiot" in the title because these may only serve to reinforce students' insecurities. Instead, they recommend making the following types of books available:

> a dictionary
> a standard encyclopedia
> an up-to-date world atlas
> writing manuals, like the *MLA Handbook for Writers*, Kate Turabian's *Manual for Writers*, the *Publication Manual of the American Psychological Association*, and William Strunk Jr., and E. B. White's *Elements of Style*
> research-paper how-to guides
> *Fowler's Modern English Usage*
> local and state histories
> international language materials as appropriate (Brannon and Hildreth 2011, 20–21)

Some libraries also carry textbooks, particularly in jurisdictions where students are not allowed to bring their schoolbooks home. The Saint Paul Public Library, for instance, buys copies of local school texts. On the other hand, more and more school districts are making books available online. Students in Santa Maria and Seattle come to the library to access their texts virtually. In Cuyahoga County, library staff have found that teachers are moving away from textbooks altogether and instead are assigning worksheets, especially for younger students.

## COMMON CORE

Although the Common Core State Standards (CCSS) seem not to have impacted public libraries as dramatically as originally feared, CCSS does continue to influence some after-school homework programs. For example, the New York Public

Library explicitly created its Enrichment Zones to help younger students improve their math and reading skills. The NYPL also offers Innovation Lab activities to develop middle school students' problem-solving and critical-thinking skills, both key Common Core elements. Other libraries have pulled together tools to help facilitate the navigation of CCSS subject areas and components. In Palos Verdes, library staff designed SchooLinks, a website that connects teachers to lesson-planning resources. A parallel homework site leads sixth and seventh graders to information on pirates, the Silk Road, major world religions, and the early Americas.[1]

The single most universally relevant aspect of Common Core is its focus on the written word. Under CCSS, traditional textbooks are heavily supplemented—and, in some schools, completely replaced—by informational resources that encourage students to think critically. High school students, in particular, are expected to read and analyze content that is based on well-researched evidence and complex concepts. While "English language arts texts" challenge young people to build knowledge, gain insights, explore possibilities, and broaden their perspective, math texts require students to apply mathematics to real-world issues, prompting them to analyze empirical situations and ultimately improve their decision making.

When selecting materials to support Common Core homework assignments, library staff should look for content that incorporates

> *Complexity* to help students comprehend increasingly complicated and sophisticated texts. Library materials should not only invite young people to read content more closely, but also challenge them to think.
> *Text structure* that encourages students to read and compare works organized in different ways (for example, by subject versus chronologically). Library materials should present alternative formatting approaches to topics.
> *Multiple perspectives* that allow students to address topics from differing points of view and that identify author bias. Library materials should either present a range of arguments or contrast other works in the collection.
> A *strong narrative* that inspires students to read and digest more nonfiction. Content should be well-written, engaging, thought-provoking, and significant.
> *Evidence-based* data—that is, arguments that are accurate, relevant, and based on research, as demonstrated through endnotes, bibliographies, appendixes, and supporting graphic images.

The Common Core Standards also require students to consult texts of "recognized value" as exhibited in primary sources. Libraries should provide access to historical documents and acknowledged "classics" as well as contemporary works that embody literary merit, cultural significance, and rich content.

Common Core expert Marc Aronson (2014) recommends compiling "text sets" of related materials to help promote students' critical thinking about various Common Core topics. A complex "anchor text" provides an overview of the subject, while shorter works in the set usually offer differing perspectives. The shorter "informational texts" can include magazine articles, websites, documentary film clips, audio recordings, and other books. By "clustering"—that is, physically juxtaposing related materials—librarians help students compare, contrast, and discriminate among various information sources (Aronson and Bartle 2012).

## ELECTRONIC RESOURCES

Besides print materials, many public libraries provide links to a variety of electronic resources. At the Prospect Heights Public Library in Illinois, separate web pages link to age-appropriate educational databases and websites for children and teens. The library's subscriptions include

> *The World Book Online Reference Center,* the classic online encyclopedia and reference resource
> Scholastic's *ScienceFlix,* which provides an in-depth examination of thirty scientific topics, including earth science, space, life science, health and the human body, physical science, technology, and engineering
> The *LearningExpress Library,* which features nearly 1,000 online tutorials, practice tests, and e-books related to skills-building in reading, writing, math, and basic science
> *Mango Languages,* the online product that helps users learn Spanish, French, Japanese, Portuguese, German, Mandarin Chinese, Greek, Italian, Russian, and more
> *TumbleBooks,* which provides online storybooks, puzzles, games, and language learning

Larger public libraries, like the NYPL, tend to offer a much wider array of curriculum-based resources that require library card registration to access. These include

> *Academic Search Premier,* a multidisciplinary database of over 4,600 journals
> *African American Experience,* an excellent full-text digital resource for middle, high school, and undergraduate students
> *Amazing Animals of the World,* detailing facts about where each species lives, what it eats, how it sounds, and why it might be endangered
> *American Indian Experience,* like the African American resource above, provides full-text content for middle, high school, and undergraduate students
> *BrainPOP,* animated online movies that help with school assignments
> *Contemporary Authors,* biographical coverage of more than 100,000 writers
> *CultureGrams,* country reports that deliver an insider's perspective on daily life and culture, including the history, customs, and lifestyles of the world's peoples
> *Latino American Experience,* full-text digital content for middle, high school, and undergraduate students
> *Opposing Viewpoints Resource Center,* the online version of the standard homework-help title
> *U.S. History in Context,* from the Vikings to the War on Terror
> *World History in Context,* from antiquity to the present day

Many libraries also point to vetted, free online sites from their homework-help web pages. Internet versions of classic student-friendly titles, like the *Occupational Outlook Handbook, CIA: The World Factbook, Background Notes,* and the Library of Congress's

*American Memory* are still popular with kids. In addition, SparkNotes is a free website that promises to make school assignments less confusing. Compiled by Barnes & Noble, the site includes guides, blogs, quizzes, flash cards, and abbreviated literary synopses to help students master difficult content. Topics include Shakespeare and other literature, history, philosophy, math, science, psychology, computer science, sociology, biography, economics, and U.S. government.[2]

Since math is perhaps the most challenging school subject for both students and homework helpers alike, many libraries make great use of Khan Academy, a free asynchronous website that offers practice exercises and word problems in four of the five STEAM topics: science, engineering, arts and humanities, and math. The website is organized by subject area, grade (kindergarten through twelfth), and user group (i.e., learners, teachers, and parents). Khan also offers free test preparation for college entrance exams.[3]

As helpful as these resources might be, they are worthless if students don't use them. A recent study conducted by the OCLC discovered that only 10 percent of teens use library websites to find information (De Rosa et al. 2010, 64). Intner (2011), therefore, recommends that libraries compile homework-related databases and websites on web pages that are

> › *Simple* to use and link to the required information quickly. The Brooklyn Public Library's "Homework Help for Kids" site, for instance, is arranged by broad category (e.g., language arts, math, science, social students test prep, etc.). Databases that require a library card and PIN are indicated by an asterisk.[4]
> › *Descriptive.* The Multnomah County Library's online homework center provides links to an array of websites—and books!—that support several school topics. Clicking on "Math" leads the user to a page that not only includes print and online resources, but also blog posts on topics, such as "Algebra in the real world!" The "Homework Databases" site is targeted directly at students and explains that the links listed "come from trusted sources that you and your teachers can cite with confidence."[5]
> › *Attractive.* Young people especially appreciate the use of color, graphics, and animation to enliven a website.
> › *Relevant.* Homework help sites must use language and images that are understandable and appeal to youngsters (Intner 2011, 85–87).

## ONLINE TUTORING

Since 2000, services like Tutor.com's Live Homework Help and Brainfuse's HelpNow have become mainstream public library programs. Students, who are registered cardholders, can access live tutors from home—or at the library—through the library's homework-help web page. Depending on the vendor contract, the service is usually available seven days a week, in the evening as well as after school. As Mayor Rahm Emanuel proclaimed when the Chicago Public Library first subscribed to HelpNow, "The addition of online tutoring allows us to offer . . . comprehensive library homework assistance . . . and demonstrates the city's continuing commitment and investment in our children" (City of Chicago 2013). One helper in Monterey County gratefully called online tutoring the homework center's "safety net," which staff use when they are completely stumped by a difficult homework question. For Judy Michaelson (2009), the benefits of online homework help include

> › the ability to connect with a live tutor over the Internet
> › no need for an appointment
> › access to on-demand help in core school subjects
> › homework help outside of school and library hours
> › access through library and home computers (Michaelson 2009, 25)

A Tutor.com case study also notes the advantage of being anonymous while using the service. Students can get assistance without identifying themselves, their teacher, or their school. This often makes youngsters feel more at ease when reaching out for help ("Case Study" 2013).

To connect to online tutoring, students log onto the vendor site through the library's web page. They then designate both their grade level and homework topic before being assigned a live tutor who is an expert in one or more of the subjects listed in figure 11.1. The student and tutor usually spend no more than an hour working through that day's homework problem, using chat and an online whiteboard, as needed. Brainfuse and Tutor.com also offer writing labs, where students can either get writing tips from a tutor in real time or upload an essay or report to be critiqued within twenty-four hours. In addition, Brainfuse can administer a test to help assess a student's academic strengths and weaknesses, followed by the creation of a learning plan.

Michaelson advises libraries to consider the following factors before selecting an online homework help service:

> › Tutor quality—Are the tutors as good at working with students as they are experts in their assigned fields?
> › Safety and student experience—How many students do tutors work with at any one time, and are the transactions truly anonymous? Can students print and save their chat and whiteboard transcripts?
> › Customer support—How responsive is the vendor to technical needs, and does the vendor help libraries market their homework help service?
> › Price—How are subscription costs calculated: by size of the library's target population? by usage? or by a combined formula of both?
> › Reporting structure—How often are usage reports released, and what exactly is measured? (Michaelson 2009, 26–27)

Although perhaps not as personal as face-to-face homework help, students nonetheless appreciate the assistance received by online tutors. A study conducted by the California State Library found satisfaction to be high among students receiving online homework help (Mediavilla and Walter 2008). Indeed, YALSA and RUSA

**FIGURE 11.1**

Homework help subject areas offered by online tutoring vendors

| Brainfuse *HelpNow* | Tutor.com *Live Homework Help* |
|---|---|
| Math | Basic Math |
| Pre-Algebra | Algebra |
| Algebra | Calculus |
| Pre-Calculus | Statistics |
| Calculus | Elementary Science |
| Trigonometry | Earth Science |
| Science | Biology |
| Biology | Chemistry |
| Chemistry | Physics |
| Physics | History |
| Social Studies | Government |
| Global History | Geography |
| U.S. History | Political Science |
| English Language Arts | Vocabulary |
| Reading | Grammar |
| Writing | Literature |

Compiled from Brainfuse *HelpNow* web page, www.brainfuse.com/highed/liveTutoring.asp and Tutor.com *Live Homework Help* web page, www.tutor.com/libraries/what-we-do#libsubjects.

recommend offering online tutoring, especially if in-house homework help programs are not possible (YALSA Board of Directors Meeting 2015).

**NOTES**

1. Palos Verdes Library District, "SchooLinks," www.pvld.org/schooLinks/.
2. SparkNotes, www.sparknotes.com/.
3. Khan Academy, www.khanacademy.org.
4. Brooklyn Public Library, "Homework Help for Kids," www.bklynlibrary.org/kids-teens/kidzone/homework-help-kids.
5. Multnomah County Library, "Homework Center," multcolib.org/homework-center.

# SUPPLIES AND EQUIPMENT

OST HOMEWORK PROGRAMS REQUIRE A CERTAIN AMOUNT OF SUP-
plies and equipment to be effective. Provisions may include
everything from simple school supplies to up-to-date laptops,
depending on community needs and the resources available.
A 2015 study of the Los Angeles Public Library's Student Zones
revealed that 59 percent of participants used the program's computer equipment that year, while 20 percent made use of the Zones' free school
supplies (Mediavilla 2015). Providing forgetful or low-income students with even
the most basic items, like pencils and paper, can go a long way toward helping
them complete their homework.

## STANDARD HOMEWORK SUPPLIES

Most public libraries keep scratch paper and extra pencils on hand for young
people to use after school, even if they don't offer formal homework help programs.
Libraries that do host formal programs often carry a more extensive list of supplies
needed to facilitate homework help. Among the most common items provided are

> writing implements, such as pencils, pens, markers, colored pencils, and
crayons
> erasers
> paper of various kinds, such as loose-leaf paper, typing paper, index cards,
graph paper, construction paper, Post-It Notes, and wide-lined paper for
younger students
> math supplies, such as flash cards, rulers, compasses, protractors, and
calculators
> office supplies, such as file folders, scissors, staplers, staple remover, three-
hole punch, whiteout, paper clips, tape, and glue sticks
> hand sanitizers and facial tissues (Mediavilla 2001, 47)

In addition to regular school supplies, the San Diego Public Library provides each homework location with play money and counting blocks, to reinforce math and financial literacy skills. At the San Ysidro branch, beans are used to help solve math problems because they are tactile and familiar to both kids and parents.

To organize and control the flow of items, homework supplies are usually secured in large plastic boxes that are brought out after school. Kids and homework assistants help themselves as needed. Supplies as well as curriculum-based materials can be permanently stored on a book truck and wheeled out when needed. As Brannon and Hildreth (2011) say, "Push [the cart] out from behind the Reference Desk to a table during after school hours and it's an instant homework center!" (23).

## FURNISHINGS

Few libraries can afford to dedicate permanent space to their homework centers; therefore, most programs do not require special furnishings. Indeed, Intner (2011) recommends taking an internal inventory before purchasing any new homework center furniture. Staff should ask themselves how students generally study in the library: Do they work alone or in pairs, or do several kids usually cram around available tables? Also, does the library have a stash of extra furniture and, if so, is it appropriate for the homework area or is it too drab and dreary? Some libraries may feel the need to create more elaborate student workspaces, while others just use the resources at hand (28–29). At the Los Angeles Public Library (LAPL), eye-catching blue structures, called The Quad, beckon students to do their schoolwork. On the other hand, Cuyahoga County's homework help is offered in branch community rooms, where library tables are set up for kids to use.

According to the academic librarian Lee C. Van Orsdel (2016), it doesn't take costly renovation or construction to create successful learning spaces. At her university library in Allendale, Michigan, the Mary Idema Pew Learning and Information Commons is filled with movable furniture and whiteboards. Flexible furnishing allows students to create a space that is most conducive for that day's studying. Whiteboards, in particular, can be used to reduce distractions and create privacy, in addition to helping students work through thorny assignments either individually or in groups. An effective learning space, Van Orsdel contends, "starts by embracing a radically user-centered library."

### TALKING POINTS

Providing forgetful or low-income students with even the most basic items, like pencils and paper, can go a long way toward helping them complete their homework. Providing young people with access to computers or laptops is even more helpful. When stocking the homework center with supplies and equipment, remember to

- Store office supplies in a large plastic box to control inventory and keep it organized. Sometimes all it takes is a well-stocked box of supplies to help kids complete their homework.

- Reuse old tables and chairs to furnish the homework center, if resources are limited. Attractive furniture, like the LAPL's The Quad, makes homework special, but it isn't always necessary for students who just need a quiet place to study.

- Keep library technology up-to-date. ALA has found that most low-income students have no access to high-speed Internet or digital tools at home.

## COMPUTER EQUIPMENT

According to the American Library Association (2016), digital equity has become a serious problem for low-income students who do not have access to high-speed Internet, digital tools, or the opportunity to learn how to use digital resources. As a result, many are unable to adequately succeed in school. No wonder, then, that some youngsters rely on the library's homework centers to provide access to up-to-date computer equipment. As "public geek" Phil Shapiro (2017) points out, "Public computers at libraries have become an extension of the classroom, and they're an important resource for children who don't have unfettered access to broadband at home." Kids start writing a paper at school, which, thanks to the library's access to the cloud, they can then finish at the homework center.

The Public Library Association advises that homework programs include

> › computers configured to allow downloading of licensed digital content to personal storage devices
> › computers that support the upload of electronic files for assignments
> › publication software for homework projects
> › color printers (Garcia and Nelson 2007, 56)

Ludwig and Braun (2011b) insist that technology should be flexible enough to go where the students are. They therefore recommend that libraries provide laptops to support homework completion. At the LAPL, 28 percent of kids surveyed said that having access to laptops is the best part of using the library's Student Zones. The laptops are used to "find stuff for homework," type papers, and print images or articles for assignments. Unfortunately, however, the equipment is so popular that students sometimes have to wait their turn to use it. When asked how the Student Zones could be improved, 25 percent of respondents requested more laptops (Mediavilla 2015).

At the La Habra branch in Orange County, California, homework center participants are allowed to use the program's laptops only after they complete their written schoolwork and wash their hands. A homework helper sits nearby while the kids use the equipment. No downloading is allowed without permission. In Paso Robles, youngsters sign up to use the Library Study Center's computers in thirty-minute blocks after they finish their homework. Most play educational games on the computers, though some older students do use them to type and print papers. A vast majority of kids who use the center do not have a computer at home.

Several libraries, including those in Bexley, Ohio, Long Beach, and San Diego, provide free printing and photocopying as part of their after-school homework program. In La Habra, students can make up to five free prints, while the Saint Paul Public Library provides up to thirty prints. Free printing is a big draw in Los Angeles as well, with half the Student Zone users saying they make copies through the program (Mediavilla 2015).

# SECURITY, USER EXPECTATIONS, AND RULES OF CONDUCT

M OST PUBLIC LIBRARIES STRIVE TO PROVIDE A SAFE LEARNING ENVI-
ronment after school. Still, few librarians consider their programs
completely risk-free. Libraries are, after all, public places and
therefore are vulnerable to outside influences. Nevertheless,
youngsters have to feel safe in the library or they will not return.
This means, of course, that staff must try to keep the homework
center as secure as possible, including enforcing predetermined rules of conduct
when necessary.

The intent of the library's homework program must also be made clear. Are
kids guaranteed personalized help with their schoolwork, or is the homework
center just a place to study and consult resources? To avoid false expectations and
liability concerns, administrators must carefully define the limitations as well as
the purpose of the library's homework program.

## PROGRAM SECURITY

When the library first introduced its homework help program many years ago in
Montclair, New Jersey, one young student expressed apprehension about working
with adult strangers (Adamec 1990). Although no library can ensure a completely
secure after-school environment, many do try to minimize threats through dil-
igent hiring practices and thoughtful placement of the homework center. Most
libraries require a security check or fingerprinting when appointing homework
center staff. Even volunteers may be required to complete application forms that
request information about past criminal records. In California, volunteers' names
may be checked against lists of convicted child abusers, made available through
"Megan's Law."[1]

Once appointed to work in the homework center, most staff, whether paid or
volunteer, are trained how to appropriately deal with after-school visitors. The mentoring of youngsters may be encouraged, but is never allowed outside the library's

walls. Homework staff are also forbidden from giving students a ride home. At the King County Library System, homework helpers are not allowed to be alone with students outside the public eye. For this reason, most Study Zones are held in the open library rather than in a meeting or community room. King County's homework helpers also wear brightly colored Study Zone T-shirts in order to distinguish them from other adults in the library. In Sacramento, the homework coaches wear a lanyard and name badge, so students know who to ask for assistance.

Homework programs offered on the library's open floor obviously present less of a security risk. Unfortunately, however, not all libraries have enough space to accommodate such open programs. To be safe, all homework activities conducted in the library's community room, or some other secluded area, must be staffed by library personnel or responsible volunteers at all times. At the Winters branch in Yolo County, the after-school SUCCESS program is held in a community room enclosed in glass walls. Not only is this a good way to attract students, but safety is ensured because the space is clearly visible to all passersby. In addition, staff walk students from the homework center to the library's restrooms to make sure no harm befalls them en route.

For security reasons, some libraries do not allow adults inside the homework center while youngsters are present. In Paso Robles, for example, no "outside" solo adults are allowed in the Library Study Center. Likewise, in King County, volunteer helpers are trained to retrieve library staff if an unwanted adult insists on participating in the program. Parents may even be restricted from the area, depending on the library. King County personnel have found that some students go to the library for homework help specifically to escape disruptive family dynamics. Therefore, parents are discouraged from accompanying their children into the Study Zones. An exception is made when the child has a learning disorder and the parent is needed to act as an intermediary or give support.

Although little research has been done on the topic, a recent study confirmed that public library employees occasionally encounter children who have been abused or neglected. Researcher Lynn Kysh (2013) recommends that every library have a written policy regarding suspected child abuse or neglect and that staff be adequately trained to handle these types of incidents. Study Zone helpers in King County are trained how to address any signs of suspected or visible child abuse. In such a situation, homework helpers are advised *not* to panic, act shocked, or become upset; place blame or be judgmental; probe for details; or make promises to help and not tell anyone. Instead, helpers should remain calm, listen carefully, and reassure the child. The incident must also be referred to the library manager, who then assesses the situation and contacts the appropriate authorities if necessary.

## CLARIFYING EXPECTATIONS

Staff must be careful to promote realistic outcomes when touting the benefits of the library's homework program. The Los Angeles Public Library, for instance, very clearly states on its website that its Student Zones provide "access to a quiet, safe place to study," but "helpers, volunteers, and librarians do not provide one-on-one tutoring." The site also reiterates that "results are not guaranteed."[2] The King County library includes similar language on its Study Zone frequently-asked-questions (FAQ) page, saying that it "cannot guarantee intensive, private one-on-one tutoring."[3] To avoid all pretense of tutorial assistance, many libraries choose to call their homework helpers "mentors," "coaches," "pals," "learning partners," "study buddies," or "learning guides" instead of "tutors," a term that often connotes licensed educational support that results in improved academic performance. As the Allen County Public Library explains on its homework help FAQ page, "Tutoring implies personal instruction in a subject area. Our Helpers are not teachers. They are here to help the students answer specific questions and complete specific homework assignments."[4]

Homework center staff can certainly commit to offering a variety of services as part of the library's program. These services may even include a safe and enriching after-school environment, opportunities to use various learning materials, guidance from peers or adult mentors, and limited homework assistance. But students and

their parents must also be made to understand the program's limitations. Staff should never guarantee an improvement in students' grades, nor should staff be expected to act as after-school babysitters. The 826NYC guidelines for homework help at the Williamsburg branch in Brooklyn are very specific. Although students are encouraged to feel at home, they are expected to have homework to do when they arrive at the center. If kids are not respectful of their surroundings, they will be asked to leave. The guidelines also warn parents that the program "should not be considered an alternative to daycare or babysitting services."[5]

## PROGRAM REGISTRATION

While many homework help programs are drop-in only, others require students to register before participating. Registration forms not only reserve a spot in the homework center, they can also be used to explain the program's parameters. (See appendix K for sample registration forms.) The first item on the Los Alamos homework help form reminds parents that it is their responsibility to make sure their child arrives at the library on time to meet with the homework helper. If the child misses two sessions without notifying the helper, he or she will lose the time slot and another student will be assigned. In Yolo County, the homework help provider requires parents to attend an orientation before registering their children in the SUCCESS program. Registration includes a "consent to medical treatment" form and a photo release.

**TALKING POINTS**

Libraries must make users feel safe and secure in the homework center. This is accomplished by

- Adopting established security procedures, such as conducting background checks on all personnel, both paid and volunteer; offering the homework center in a clearly visible part of the building; and restricting outside adults from participating in the program. King County also trains Study Zone staff how to handle victims of suspected child abuse.

- Clarifying the homework center's purpose and limitations on the library's website, as well as on the program registration form. Staff must be careful not to promise more than the program can deliver. In fact, some libraries avoid calling their helpers "tutors" for fear of raising false expectations.

- Requiring parental approval for youngsters to participate in the program.

- Creating and enforcing homework center rules of conduct. The most effective rules are those that avoid using the words "no" or "don't."

The Mission Viejo Library provides two registration forms: one for second through sixth graders and one for seventh through twelfth graders. For parents of younger children, the form describes the library's homework program and hours offered. There is also a disclaimer that the completion of school assignments is not guaranteed. When the parent and child sign the form, they both acknowledge that disruptive behavior will result in removal from the study room. Parents also agree that they will stay in the library for the duration of the homework help session. For older students, the form explains how to make a homework assistance appointment and specifies that helpers do not correct work or give answers to tests. The program is so popular that there is no guarantee the student will be able to see a helper during the time assigned. Participants in both Mission Viejo homework programs must be library cardholders.

The registration form for Cuyahoga County's program reminds parents that

> students will be released into the library once their homework session has ended
> the homework center provides access to the Internet
> one-on-one tutoring is not offered
> participants may be recorded and/or surveyed as part of the program's evaluation
> snacks may be provided

Parental permission is also requested to view the child's school records so homework center staff can track students' academic progress. Kids can remain in the program even if their parents refuse to release school records.[6]


## RULES OF CONDUCT

Some programs post rules of conduct for students to follow while using the homework center. The best rules are those that promote positive behaviors rather than telling kids what they should not do. In San José, both the parent and child must agree to a set of rules required of all young people participating in the library's Homework Club. The rules ask students to bring their homework and all required materials, and to work quietly and be respectful of fellow students and homework coaches.

At the Library Study Center in Paso Robles, two large and colorful hand-painted signs reinforce good after-school behavior. The first sign reminds students to

1. Treat all people and materials with RESPECT.
2. Loud voices, running, skipping, dancing, and yelling belong OUTSIDE.
3. Clean up workspace before you leave.
4. Sign in and out for computer/Wii and ask staff for supplies.

The second sign addresses homework expectations more specifically, emphasizing that

WE WILL

> Study and learn new things.
> Use appropriate language.
> Respect others.
> Be cooperative and respectful.
> Keep a positive attitude.
> And behave in a way that promotes study learning.

Although both signs hope to regulate behavior, they use positive terms to do so, instead of telling kids "no" or "don't."

**NOTES**

1. State of California Department of Justice, Office of the Attorney General, "California Megan's Law Website," www.meganslaw.ca.gov/.
2. Los Angeles Public Library, "Student Zones: The Quad," www.lapl.org/teens/homework-help/student-zones.
3. King County Library System, "Study Zone," kcls.org/study-zone/.
4. Allen County Public Library, "Homework Help Fall 2016," www.acpl.lib.in.us/home/explore/teens/notes-from-the-underground/teens/2016/09/13/homework-help-fall-2016.
5. 826NYC, "After-School," 826nyc.org/program/afterschool/.
6. Cuyahoga County Public Library, "Homework Centers Registration Form," www.cuyahogalibrary.org/getmedia/583430b0-da50-49bf-9b2b-b450f15ef2d6/HomeworkCenter2016registration.pdf.aspx.

# MEDIA AND PUBLIC RELATIONS

EVEN THE BEST HOMEWORK HELP PROGRAMS NEED PUBLICITY TO ATTRACT users. As Annie Poyner, coordinator of King County's Study Zones, has observed, it can take up to three years for public library homework centers to get fully off the ground. The California State Library made a similar discovery after it launched its statewide out-of-school time online homework help project, and so it decided to provide three years of support to libraries participating in the program. Though students have been using library materials to do research for more than 100 years, most community members do not think of the public library as a source for one-on-one homework help. Therefore, a public relations campaign is necessary.

The early teen services advocate Stan Weisner (1992) recommends using several strategies to advertise library programs. These include

› developing and publicizing newsworthy special events and activities
› preparing user-friendly publicity materials
› using existing communications channels whenever possible

Regardless of the method, the library's publicity should target parents, teachers, volunteers, funding agencies, and governing bodies, as well as students—for without the support of all these groups, the homework center will not succeed.

## SPECIAL EVENTS AND RECOGNITION

One of the most newsworthy events the library can stage is a "grand opening" or ribbon-cutting ceremony, where the community is invited to see firsthand what exactly the homework center looks like and does. This can also offer the perfect opportunity for local politicians to witness how much their constituents value the library. San Diego's Do Your Homework @ the Library program was launched at the Logan Heights branch, serving one of the city's most diverse communities.

Present at the event were the mayor, the city council president, a council member, the school district superintendent, the library foundation's chair, and the city librarian (Chamberlayne 2014). In Saint Paul, the mayor kicked off the 2016/17 school year at an open house at the busy Rondo branch library's homework center. Describing the public library as "instrumental in supporting the academic success of our students," the mayor went on to note that the homework program "fosters out-of-school time learning and helps our youth both in and outside the classroom." He then distributed school supplies to kids attending the event.[1]

At a minimum, the library should work with the governing body's information office to generate a media release about the new homework help service. The best coverage will feature enthusiastic quotes from leading government officials as well as library authorities. When Chicago's Teacher in the Library program was expanded to all branch sites in 2013, the news was announced from Mayor Rahm Emanuel's office, under a headline proclaiming that the library now offers the largest homework help program in the nation. "Opportunities to learn shouldn't stop when the school bell rings," the mayor was quoted as saying. "Teacher in the Library offers students an added resource to receive help with their studies at libraries across the city" (City of Chicago 2013).

Media releases and launch events should also recognize the contributions made by donors and other funders. When the Eli and Edythe Broad Foundation decided to donate $1 million to support the Los Angeles Public Library's Student Zones program, the library, the library's foundation, and the school district all happily announced the generous gift. "We are thrilled that the Broad Foundation is investing in young Angelenos through the Los Angeles Public Library," city librarian John Szabo told a writer for the *L.A. School Report*. "Students across the city rely on their neighborhood branch libraries as an extension of their academics, taking advantage of services such as our online tutoring . . . and this gift will allow us to further our efforts to help every student succeed" (Favot 2016).

## USER-FRIENDLY PUBLICITY

Of course, not all public relations efforts are focused on the launching of new homework help services. Once the program gets under way, students, teachers, and families may need to be reminded that the homework center exists. Distributing library-generated flyers is one of the most popular, effective, and least expensive ways of advertising homework programs. Well-designed flyers include information about the purpose of the program, its location, hours of service, telephone number, website, and intended audience. Intner (2011) suggests posting flyers near water fountains, in public bathrooms, on tables in the youth services area, inside homework-related library books, and under the flap of the library's photocopy machines. Outside the library, she recommends placing flyers in local businesses that students frequent, including movie theaters, coffee shops, bookstores, mall food courts, candy shops, and even health clubs (148).

Eye-catching trinkets emblazoned with the homework center's name, logo, telephone number, and website can also be effective in attracting potential users. The King County library distributes Study Zone pencils and has translated its brochure into seven languages. Parents especially appreciate magnets that can be easily displayed on the kitchen refrigerator. Promotional magnets should include homework center locations, hours, and telephone numbers.

Even though Suellen S. Adams (2010) acknowledges the value of traditional promotional strategies, such as brochures, media releases, giveaways, and flyers, she encourages library staff to also market their homework programs through digital means. Perhaps the most ubiquitous method is via well-placed and well-designed websites. Unfortunately, many homework help links are buried on the library's teen and/or children's services web pages. The best homework center websites are those that are easy to find and provide a description of the program and its guidelines, as well as center locations, hours, and links to the registration form (if required). Excellent website examples include Cuyahoga County, LAPL's Student Zones, and Mission Viejo.[2] Boston's stellar homework-help web page also links to other programs outside the library.[3] The most thorough homework center site, however, is King County's Study Zone web page, which provides an extensive FAQ that lists the following information:

> What is the Study Zone schedule?
> What is a Study Zone?
> Who can attend Study Zone?
> What subjects can I get help in?
> Do tutors have skills in languages besides English?
> What do I need to bring to Study Zone?
> How do I join Study Zone?
> How much does it cost?
> Who are the tutors?[4]

The website lets King County residents know exactly what services the Study Zones offer and where to find them.

## EXISTING COMMUNICATIONS CHANNELS

RUSA and YALSA urge public libraries to collaborate with partner organizations to promote the library's homework help services and resources (YALSA Board of Directors Meeting 2015, 2). Indeed, library staff should make use of existing communications channels whenever possible. Chamber of commerce newsletters, parent-teacher association bulletins, Friends of the Library publications, church circulars, home-owner-association newsletters, and monthly water and power

### TALKING POINTS

Because awareness of the homework center can take as much as three years to completely penetrate the community, a media strategy should be devised to thoroughly promote the program. Tried-and-true publicity techniques include

- Special events to celebrate the grand opening of the homework center. Invite government officials to attend and say a few words, so they can be quoted in the newspaper and other media outlets.

- Low-cost but high-impact methods, such as web pages and printed flyers. Eye-catching designs should be informative as well as attractive, describing the program's location, purpose, and benefits.

- Word of mouth via existing contacts, community partners, and the students themselves. If popular group leaders start using the program, other kids will soon follow.

bills are all good outlets for free publicity. Word of mouth can also be a powerful public relations tool. In fact, Intner (2011) recommends asking kids directly to promote the library's homework center to their friends (156–57). At the Dacula branch of the Gwinnett County Library, attendance suddenly spiked once teen group leaders started getting homework help. Peer endorsement goes a long way in attracting young people to the library.

Intner also suggests working closely with local schools to promote the program. Teachers, in particular, can be strong allies if they know they can refer students to the library for hands-on homework help (149–50). The Allen County Library sends posters and informational bookmarks to the local middle and high schools to advertise its teen homework service. The library also promotes the program to parents through the school district's electronic newsletter. In Chicago, library staff send promotional postcards to parents through the schools once classes start in the fall. Adams (2010) strongly recommends adding a link from the school's web page to the library's homework center website, if at all possible. Because the school's web page is a hub for all school-related information, providing a link from there to the homework center will no doubt raise awareness of the library's program as yet another educational resource.

## NOTES

1. "Mayor Coleman Kicks Off the School Year," YouTube video, www.youtube.com/watch?v =6aLnQXkivak.
2. Cuyahoga County Public Library, "Homework Help," www.cuyahogalibrary.org/homework .aspx; Los Angeles Public Library, "Student Zones: The Quad," www.lapl.org/teens/ homework-help/student-zones; and Mission Viejo Library, "Homework Help & Tutoring," cityofmissionviejo.org/departments/library/library-services/homework-help-tutoring.
3. Boston Public Library, "Homework Help," www.bpl.org/homework/.
4. King County Library System, "Study Zone," kcls.org/study-zone/.

# EVALUATION AND MEASURING OUTCOMES

T
WENTY-FIVE YEARS AGO, ROSELLEN BREWER (1992) WISELY OBSERVED that librarians must find a way to measure the effectiveness of homework help programs if they are to continue. Still, only a handful of libraries evaluate their homework services today. Certainly staff, who work with students, observe and intuitively understand the value of formal homework assistance. But funders as well as governing bodies need more concrete evidence to justify continued support. Targeting homework-help outcomes that are then measured to show what has been achieved is a compelling way to demonstrate program effectiveness.

## OUTCOME-BASED HOMEWORK HELP PROGRAMS

Outcomes are the benefits derived from using the library's services. Typically these benefits result in positive changes in one's attitude, behavior, skills, knowledge, condition, or status. For example, evidence of outcome achievement might be apparent in adolescent immigrants who suddenly understand the rules of English grammar (i.e., a gain in knowledge) or in children who diligently do their homework instead of running around the library and causing havoc (i.e., a positive change in behavior). Although both these scenarios are hypothetical, they are based on very real situations that homework centers address every day. By targeting and measuring the specific benefits of the homework help experience, the library demonstrates that it provides a valuable service worthy of the continued support of community members and funders alike.

When measuring achievement of its "Succeed in School: Homework Help" service response, the Public Library Association recommends considering an array of outcomes to target:

> › number and percent of specified students who improve their reading skills
> › number and percent of specified students who improve their writing skills

> number and percent of specified students who improve their math skills
> number and percent of specified students who improve their grades
> number and percent of specified students who increase their enjoyment of learning
> number and percent of specified students who complete their year/graduate from school
> number and percent of specified students who achieve a personal goal associated with success in school (Garcia and Nelson 2007, 56)

Though no library can tackle all of these outcomes in a single academic year, any of these statements, on their own, are indicators of student success and so are valid benchmarks for the Succeed in School service response. Moreover, any one or more of these outcomes could provide the inspiration for creating a public library homework center.

The Chicago Public Library targets three types of outcomes for its Teacher in the Library program: short-term, intermediate, and long-term. The expected outcomes are described below.

## Short-Term

> Children view the library as a safe and supportive environment for completing homework assignments.
> Parents/caregivers view the library as a resource to help them support their children in after-school learning.

## Intermediate

> Completion of homework assignments
> Improved social and communication skills
  — Development of positive relationships with adults (parent, teacher, and librarian)
> Improved attitudes towards homework and after-school learning

## Long-Term

> Improved work habits during after-school hours
  — Children show increased confidence in themselves as learners ("TIL/Homework Help Logic Model" 2016)

## OUTCOME STATEMENTS

These outcome statements not only inform what services are offered as part of the Teacher in the Library program, they are also the benchmarks that measure success. Indeed, at the end of the school year, students and their parents are surveyed to ascertain whether or not the outcomes were achieved. In 2014, for instance, 87 percent of participants reported that they felt better about doing homework, while 84 percent said they felt more confident about themselves as learners. Seventy-four percent of students also responded that they felt more comfortable talking to adults as a result of participating in Teacher in the Library. In addition, 95 percent of parents indicated that their kids had an improved attitude toward homework as well as improved after-school work habits. Parents also reported that their children showed a better attitude toward school. Although these findings address only a few of the stated outcomes, one can already conclude that the library achieved its goals and that, based on these results, Teacher in the Library is an effective homework help program ("Teacher in the Library Survey Results" 2014).

## MEASURING ACHIEVEMENT

Satisfactory attainment of the library's anticipated homework help outcomes is measured through evaluation. Although it is sometimes difficult to isolate variables directly attributable to the effectiveness of after-school services, the program evaluator should be able to assess whether the homework center is

> › accomplishing its stated outcome(s)
> › reaching its target population
> › having a positive impact on the students served

The evaluator should also be able to decipher the quantity and quality of the homework assistance offered as part of the program.

In our book on outcome-based planning and evaluation of public library programs, Melissa Gross, Virginia Walter, and I present a hypothetical case study where community assessment reveals the need to help middle school students pass math. To address the situation, we have library staff target an outcome that will result in middle school students comprehending math homework. This then leads to the creation of a weekly math tutoring session in the library. Success is measured through a combination of methods, including counting the number of math assignments completed, as well as the number of participants who pass their math class at the end of the school year. Library staff also survey the students, their parents, and the math tutors to see exactly what was accomplished (Gross, Mediavilla, and Walter 2016).

RUSA and YALSA recommend that libraries use both quantitative and qualitative methods to evaluate homework help programs. Quantitative data include the amount of space and pieces of equipment used to deliver the program, the number of people who participate, and other use statistics to determine whether the homework center's core requirements are being met. Qualitative data, on the other hand, include anecdotal evidence, student self-reports, secret shopper observations, and survey data that indicate what skills and knowledge have been acquired (YALSA Board of Directors Meeting 2015, 3).

## MEASURING QUANTITY

One of the most common statistics gathered by homework center staff is daily usage. Even drop-in programs may require students to sign in, so daily head counts can be tabulated. Tracking these head counts not only shows how much the program is used, but can also help managers determine how many volunteers are needed to staff the center on certain days of the week. Equally important is the number of unique visitors who seek homework help either multiple times a year or just once. A statistic claiming that 2,400 students use the homework center may be impressive, but funders, in particular, will want to know whether these are individual users or the same fifteen kids visiting the center every day it's open.

Walter (1995) estimates that 20 percent of homework center participants account for 80 percent of the program's use (52). While a high percentage of repeat customers may seem to indicate satisfaction, these figures can be deceptive, especially in latchkey situations where kids have nowhere else to go. It is therefore recommended that libraries keep a record of all their homework center users, even if the service is drop-in only. The San Diego Public Library's homework program, for example, requires students to sign in every day, including first and last name, birthdate, grade, school, homework topic(s), whether this is the first time using the library (yes/no), and time in and out of the center. To track unique visits, staff assign each child an internal identification number based on the student's initials and birthdate and then tally attendance accordingly. During the 2015/16 academic year, nearly 4,200 San Diego students visited the library's homework centers a total of 18,262 times. Of these, 61 percent used the program only once (San Diego Public Library 2016).

In addition to head counts, some libraries also collect data on how the homework center is used. School-related Internet use may be tracked to justify the purchase of extra homework-help computers and laptops, while staff may want to log homework reference questions to map their relevance to the library's collection. Using a "homework fill rate" form helps determine whether requested titles and subjects are on the shelf. A low "fill rate" may indicate a need to review the library's collection in light of the local school curriculum (Walter 1995, 62–67).

Twice a year, the Los Angeles Public Library asks Student Zone participants how and why they use the library's homework help service. In 2015/16, 95 percent of respondents said they use Student Zone resources to complete their homework or school projects. More specifically they use the library's computers to access the Internet (56 percent), make free prints (56 percent), and type an essay or research paper (51 percent). Another 51 percent of the kids said they use the space to study. The library also asks for limited demographic information to determine exactly who uses the service. Although a nearly equal number of males and females participate in the program, it is interesting to note that users are predominantly students of color, with 51 percent self-identifying as Latino, 18 percent African American,

9 percent Asian, and 9 percent multiracial. Only 2 percent said they were white (Library Foundation of Los Angeles 2016).

The number of hours worked by volunteer helpers, as well as overall center service hours, should also be tallied to confirm the scope of the program. Repeat pairings between a particular homework helper and student may indicate a successful working relationship. On the other hand, a large student-to-helper ratio may validate the need for more homework assistance. In San Diego, the library's after-school homework program provided a total of 22,329 hours of assistance at 18 sites during the 2015/16 school year. Individual participants each averaged five hours of homework help throughout the year (San Diego Public Library 2016).

## MEASURING QUALITY

Many libraries assess the effectiveness of their homework centers simply through observation and anecdotal evidence. For these libraries, success is measured by the number of smiles that greet homework staff every day or by the look of comprehension that suddenly appears on a student's face. At one library, the administrator knew staff had performed well when a fourth-grade teacher came in to witness for herself the homework program her students had praised so highly.

Sharing anecdotes can be a powerful way to humanize quantitative data. Heartfelt stories about library staff connecting with high school students go a long way toward illustrating the quality of the Seattle Public Library's homework help program. Yet qualitative data are even more meaningful when collected through formal means, such as staff reports, surveys, or focus groups. In Sacramento, one teen homework helper created a blog to record her experiences assisting youngsters with their schoolwork. She also sought input from parents and fellow homework helpers, ultimately providing a marvelous snapshot of what the Belle Cooledge branch's homework program was really like (Kong 2016). Written testimonials like this one can provide a meaningful context for otherwise mundane attendance figures.

Most libraries conduct some sort of survey to help evaluate their homework center. Surveys are easy and inexpensive to administer, can be completed anonymously, and generate lots of data. When using them to help evaluate homework programs, surveys are typically run once a year and tend to collect feedback from parents as well as their kids. (See appendix L for sample survey instruments.) Although some questions are more quantitative—such as "How often do you use the homework center?" or "What kind of homework do

### TALKING POINTS

Despite acknowledging the need for and the value of program evaluation, few libraries actually measure the effectiveness of their homework help services. When arguing in favor of evaluating homework centers, the following should be emphasized:

- Quantitative data are important when capturing workload. Even more powerful, however, are qualitative data that measure the positive impact of the program. Big numbers may impress, but funders and governing bodies will also want to know how the homework center made a difference in students' lives.

- When collecting quantitative data, be sure to differentiate between total transactions and individual users. Both figures are informative yet distinctly different. Funders as well as library administrators will want to know exactly how many people use the service.

- Evaluation based on community-specific outcomes is a compelling way to demonstrate program effectiveness. But sometimes it's just easier to borrow outcome statements that have already been tested elsewhere. Although the PLA's Project Outcomes initiative is still relatively new, the concept of measuring the nationwide impact of educational public library programs is attractive and worthy of further exploration.

you need the most help with?"—others are qualitative, attempting to capture user satisfaction or more affective responses. Satisfaction-based questions aimed at students usually ask

> what the youngster likes most about the program
> whether staff are helpful
> whether the homework center is the best place to get academic help outside of school
> what would make the program better
> whether the student would recommend the program to friends

When gauging parent satisfaction, libraries might ask

> how effective staff are in providing homework help
> what the parent likes about the program
> whether there are enough staff and volunteers to help students
> whether the parent would recommend the program to other parents

Surveys are also commonly used to measure the positive impact of the homework center. Depending on the library's targeted outcomes, staff may ask students if they now

> understand their homework better
> get better grades
> complete their homework
> are more organized
> feel more comfortable talking to adults
> feel better about doing homework
> have better work habits
> feel more confident as a learner
> feel better about school

Parents might also be asked to assess a change in their child's attitude, skill, knowledge, or behavior as a result of using the homework center. Questions posed could include

> Does your child now understand homework better?
> Have your child's grades improved?
> Does your child have a better attitude about school?
> Are evenings at home now less stressful regarding school assignments?
> Does your child spend more time doing homework?
> Does your child feel comfortable at the homework center?
> Has participating in the homework center helped your child learn to interact well with other children?
> Have staff given you guidance, resources, or support to help you work with your child on school assignments?

Libraries should also consider surveying their homework helpers. They do, after all, spend the most "face time" with program participants. At the end of the school year, the Solano County Library solicits direct input from its helpers, asking for feedback on the strengths of the program as well as its weaknesses. These data are then used to plan the following year's homework program. Likewise, in 2015, I surveyed the Student Zone helpers for a study I conducted for the Los Angeles Public Library. I asked them

> what happens on a typical day at their Student Zone
> what benefits they think students derive from participating in the program
> what skills and knowledge they themselves have acquired as a result of helping kids with their homework
> how the program has influenced their future career plans
> what challenges they had to overcome when working at the Student Zone

Their input provided an especially unique perspective on a service that impacts many young people daily.

Besides surveys, some libraries have found focus groups to be an effective way of gathering qualitative feedback about the homework program. A focus group, of course, is nothing more than a group interview with some six to twelve people who have something in common (e.g., age, gender, socioeconomic background, parental status, language, etc.). Students who regularly use the homework center might be asked to meet for fifteen to thirty minutes to discuss the program and suggest areas for improvement. Focus groups should be conducted by a neutral and, if necessary, bilingual facilitator in a casual, nonthreatening environment where light refreshments can be served. Questions should be open-ended to avoid one-word answers. Walter (1995) suggests asking kids

> what kinds of homework they do while using the homework center
> why they use the homework center
> what they like best about the program
> how the program can be improved (83)

The California Library Association, which advocates measuring the outcomes of summer reading clubs, has developed an extensive list of guidelines for leading effective focus groups. They recommend training teens to conduct sessions with younger kids, and giving participants—adults and children alike—paper and drawing materials to doodle with during the session. Facilitators should focus on asking questions and listening to responses, while a second person takes notes. Also, parents should be notified before the focus group interviews their children. Staff might want to emphasize that the focus group is an enrichment experience and an opportunity for the child to give feedback to the library. And, of course, the library should always provide food.[1]

## BORROWING OUTCOME STATEMENTS

As Intner (2011) has argued, for any evaluation to be valid, it must have a base or standard against which change is measured (160). The Hennepin County Library (2016b), for instance, has targeted three explicit outcomes for its after-school homework centers:

› Youth develop and improve twenty-first-century learning skills (critical thinking, problem-solving, basic literacy, and mathematical thinking) more than if they did not come to Homework Help.
› Youth gain confidence in their abilities and experience increased motivation to do well in school by connecting with caring adult mentors.
› Library staff have a better understanding of who uses Homework Help, why, and their capacity to meet the demands.

Not only do these goals inform the design of the library's program, they also serve as the benchmarks against which the service is measured. In 2015/16, Hennepin County conducted an extensive evaluation of its homework centers. Using surveys, it discovered that 60 percent of students always understand their school assignments better after visiting the library's homework centers. Moreover, 92 percent do better on their homework because of the help received from the library's mentors, and 79 percent now want to learn new things. Homework helpers, who were also surveyed, confirm the success of the program. "I can see lightbulbs go off in their heads when there is a learning moment and a large smile follows," one volunteer shared. "That's confidence happening right before my eyes" (Hennepin County Library 2016b).

Designating and then creating services to meet outcomes that address the community's unique priorities is, of course, preferable to using someone else's goals. However, sometimes it's just easier to borrow outcomes that have already been tested elsewhere. Several years ago, Virginia Walter and I used elements of the Search Institute's (2017) "40 Developmental Assets" to study the impact of homework help programs on teens. In particular, we examined whether homework services provided by libraries result in the following six asset-based outcomes:

› Youth contribute to their community.
› They feel safe in their environment.
› They have meaningful relationships with adults and peers.
› They achieve educational success.
› They develop marketable skills.
› They develop personal and social skills.

We found that not only were these outcomes achievable, but any of them would provide an effective framework for designing and evaluating homework help programs for teens (Walter and Mediavilla 2003; Walter and Meyers 2003, 93–97). Indeed, libraries would do well using one or more of these to launch their own homework service.

In 2015 the Public Library Association released Project Outcome, a platform for measuring and analyzing the impact of public library services nationwide. This field-tested initiative provides a template for creating outcome statements and makes available free, standardized survey instruments that measure services in seven broad areas, including education and lifelong learning. People participating in the library's educational programs are surveyed about whether they

> learned something new that is helpful
> feel more confident about what was just learned
> intend to apply what was just learned
> are now more aware of applicable resources and services provided by the library

More in-depth follow-up questions ask whether program participants used what was learned to complete a task or goal and/or do something new or different.

Although Project Outcome does not address after-school homework help specifically, it does provide a framework for evaluating the effectiveness of educational programs that improve academic performance. Libraries that participate in the project submit their data to the PLA, which then aggregates the findings to create a national profile of public library service impact. In 2016, 94 percent of survey respondents who participated in an educational or lifelong learning event at their library said they learned something new and helpful (Public Library Association 2016).

**NOTE**

1. California Summer Reading Challenge, "Focus Groups," calchallenge.org/evaluation/out comes/focus-groups/.

# Model Homework Programs

| **PROGRAM** | **LIBRARY** |
|---|---|
| Homework Help | Boston Public Library, Boston, Massachusetts |

**CONTACT PERSON**

Angela Veizaga, Systemwide Youth Programs Librarian

617-859-2198

aveizaga@bpl.org

**PROGRAM WEB PAGE**

www.bpl.org/homework/

**HOURS**

Monday through Thursday, 3:30 to 5:30 PM

**FUNDING SOURCE**

Part of the library's regular budget.

**STAFFING**

The program is staffed by high-achieving high school students, who are hired and trained to provide homework assistance.

**TARGET POPULATION**

Kindergarteners through eighth graders

**PURPOSE**

Provide after-school homework help at several branches throughout Boston.

**SPECIAL FEATURES**

Started in 2000, the Boston Public Library's drop-in Homework Help program has a well-established and successful track record of assisting students with their school assignments. Seventeen library branches currently offer the program after school. Homework assistance is provided by more than fifty high-achieving high school student mentors, who have a grade-point-average of 3.0 or higher. Some of the teens are bilingual, speaking Vietnamese, Spanish, and East African languages as well as English. Training is conducted by Harvard University's Teaching and Learning Partnerships team, which instructs the mentors on how to use SmartTALK, a structured yet fun method of supporting academic success. Smart-TALK focuses on the effective use of homework time by transitioning kids to game-related learning after finishing that day's school assignment. Helping develop students' organizational, study, problem-solving, and collaborative skills is also emphasized. Throughout the process, youngsters strengthen relationships with their teachers as well as the mentors. Besides learning how to implement the SmartTALK technique, Homework Help mentors are encouraged to apply to participate in a special leadership program offered by Harvard. Four teens are selected and help train their fellow mentors throughout the academic year.

In addition to Homework Help, the library also hosts tutoring sessions offered by members of the Boston Teachers Union at twenty-four branches. All students are welcome to participate. The schedule varies by branch site.

---

**PROGRAM**
Teacher in the Library

**LIBRARY**
Chicago Public Library, Chicago, Illinois

**CONTACT PERSON**
Elizabeth McChesney, System Wide Children's Services Director
312-747–4784
emcchesn@chipublib.org

**PROGRAM WEB PAGE**
https://www.chipublib.org/news/free-homework-help/

**HOURS**
Weekday afternoons, Monday through Thursday. Specific days and hours vary by branch site.

**FUNDING SOURCE**
Chicago Public Library Foundation

**STAFFING**
Credentialed teachers, who are placed in the library through a human resources agency.

**TARGET POPULATION**
All students, ages three through nineteen, are welcome.

**PURPOSE**
Accredited teachers help students build good study habits and increase their academic confidence.

**SPECIAL FEATURES**
Piloted in just six sites in 2000, some fifty teachers now rotate among the library's eighty branches, helping kids with their homework and, in many cases, serving as mentors. At one branch, the teacher is very active in helping high school students acquire scholarships. Some teachers walk around the library and ask youngsters if they need assistance, while others take a seat and wait for students to approach them. Over 30,000 children are helped by Teacher in the Library every year. Several of the teachers are bilingual, speaking the Spanish, Urdu, Farsi, Japanese, and Hindi languages, in addition to English.

Besides teachers, who are paid for their services, the library also recruits volunteer helpers who have expertise in particular subjects. The volunteers provide homework help on Sunday, at three branches, as well as during the week. Online homework help is also provided by the library's subscription to Brainfuse's HelpNow.

The program is evaluated through an outcome-based logic model that uses both qualitative and quantitative data to measure effectiveness. The completion of school assignments, improved social and communication skills, development of positive relationships with adults, improved attitude toward after-school learning, improved work habits, and increased confidence in themselves as learners are all targeted outcomes for Teacher in the Library students. In 2012, Teacher in the Library was recognized as an innovative education program by the Urban Libraries Council.

**PROGRAM**
Homework Centers
Homework Mentors

**LIBRARY**
Cuyahoga County Public Library
Cuyahoga County, Ohio

**CONTACT**
Julia Boxler, Youth Programming Manager
216-749–9401
jboxler@cuyahogalibrary.org

**PROGRAM WEB PAGE**
www.cuyahogalibrary.org/homework.aspx

**HOURS**
Homework Centers are offered in two shifts, 4:00 to 5:15 PM and 5:15 to 6:30 PM, Monday through Thursday.
Homework Mentors are available after school for two hours, Monday through Thursday. Times vary by branch site.

**FUNDING SOURCE**
Both programs are funded through various foundations, including the Cleveland Foundation. Federal funds pay for America Reads work-study homework helpers.

**STAFFING**
Temporary seasonal workers coordinate the Homework Center at each site. They supervise the homework helpers, who are either volunteers or paid library staff, as well as the America Reads work-study students. The homework mentors are also temporary seasonal employees.

**TARGET POPULATION**
The programs are aimed at kindergarteners through eighth graders, though both programs are used primarily by seven- through ten-year-olds.

## PURPOSE
Homework Centers is a structured program that provides homework, reading, and math assistance, followed by educational games and activities.
Homework Mentors provide homework assistance as needed.

## SPECIAL FEATURES
Originally called Youth Experience Success (Y.E.S.), the Cuyahoga County Library's homework help service started in 2002 thanks to a $1,000 grant from Sam's Club. Since then, the Homework Centers, located in ten branches, have assisted thousands of children with their schoolwork. Homework Center sessions are scheduled twice a day in 75-minute shifts. Up to twenty-five kids can participate and must be preregistered by their parents, even though the program is drop-in only. Children receive homework help or reading and math assistance, followed by twenty minutes of reading practice and twenty minutes of educational games or activities. Homework help is provided by a mix of library staff, volunteers, and trained America Reads tutors from local colleges and universities. Most Homework Center sites have a dedicated space for homework help. Depending on that day's class assignments, students complete their homework before rotating among reading, educational games, keyboarding, or other academic activities.

The Homework Mentor program is offered in fourteen branches that do not have Homework Centers. In this much less structured service, the homework mentor roves around the building, asking kids if they need help with their homework.

---

## PROGRAM
Study Zones

## LIBRARY
King County Library System,
King County, Washington

## CONTACT PERSON
Annie Poyner, Public Services Specialist
425-369–3312
apoyner@kcls.org

## PROGRAM WEB PAGE
www.kcls.org/studyzone

## HOURS
Hours vary by site, Sunday through Saturday

## FUNDING SOURCES
The program is part of the library's budget, which is often offset by donations made specifically in support of the Study Zones program.

### STAFFING

A part-time public services specialist coordinates the overall program, which is managed at each branch by the teen services librarian. Homework help is provided by volunteers, who reflect the diversity of their communities.

### TARGET POPULATION

The program is open to all kindergarteners through twelfth-grade students working on any level of homework, plus anyone up to twenty-one years old doing kindergarten through twelfth-grade level coursework, including preparing for the general education degree (GED).

### PURPOSE

The program provides a place for students to study, do homework, and get help with their questions from volunteer helpers.

### SPECIAL FEATURES

Possibly the largest public library homework help program in the country, the Study Zones were launched in the early 2000s and have inspired the creation of homework centers across the United States and even in Japan. Volunteer helpers must be at least sixteen years old and either a junior or senior in high school. Only 25 percent of the program's 300 volunteers are teens. The rest are adults of all ages, many of whom have been with the program for several years. Service is rewarded with a special certificate at five, ten, fifteen, and twenty years. One older woman, who just started volunteering, said it's a lot easier helping strangers do their homework than it was helping her own daughter!

Reflecting the diversity of the area, the homework helpers speak fourteen languages other than English. These include Korean, Hindi, Chinese, Russian, Spanish, Tamil, Farsi, Latin, Japanese, Vietnamese, Somali, French, Arabic, and German. A list of bilingual helpers and their branch locations is posted on the Study Zone web page. A list of homework helpers by subject expertise is also posted. Homework topics include all levels of mathematics, accounting, biology, chemistry, physics, English, history, reading, and computer skills.

Students typically use the program if their parents work or if there are language or education barriers at home. Foster care and homeless kids especially like the Study Zones because they are consistent, easily accessed at most King County branches, and completely anonymous. Over 13,700 hours of homework help were delivered in 2014/15.

---

### PROGRAM
Student Zones

### LIBRARY
Los Angeles Public Library (LAPL)
Los Angeles, California

### CONTACT PERSONS
Candice Mack, Senior Librarian, Young Adult Services
213-228-7370 | yasvcs@lapl.org
Imani Harris, Director, Foundation and Corporate Relations
213-292-6243 | imaniharris@lfla.org

## PROGRAM WEB PAGE
www.lapl.org/teens/homework-help/student-zones

## HOURS
Monday through Thursday, 2:30 to 6:00 PM

## FUNDING SOURCE
Library Foundation of Los Angeles

## STAFFING
The library's youth services department oversees the Student Zones with support from the Library Foundation of Los Angeles. With the assistance and supervision of library staff, Student Zone helpers are recruited and trained through PowerMyLearning, a national nonprofit organization dedicated to improving educational outcomes through the power of digital learning.

## TARGET POPULATION
The program is aimed at low-income youth, though all kindergarten through twelfth-grade students are welcome.

## PURPOSE
The program's purpose is to provide access to a quiet, safe place to study and receive the guidance needed to succeed in school.

## SPECIAL FEATURES
One-on-one homework assistance is provided at thirty-four LAPL branches located throughout the city of Los Angeles. Of these, twenty branches offer The Quad, a self-contained and distinct space where young people can study and complete class assignments. Furnished with a comfortable sofa, chairs, and ergonomically appropriate computer tables, the bright blue Quads are a cool place for kids to hang out after school. The Quad brand is a play on the words "quadrangle," an open space common on college campuses, and "quadrilateral," a four-sided polygon. Though located on the library's open floor, the Quad's eye-catching design is attractive to students who have made the space their own. Laptops and tablets are also made available to Student Zone users. All school assignment-related photocopies and printing are free.

The program is a stellar example of what can be accomplished when a library and its foundation work together to achieve a common goal. The Student Zones were initially piloted in a handful of branches and then slowly expanded as need was identified. Among the program's biggest supporters is the Eli and Edythe Broad Foundation, a generous donor well known for supporting the arts and education across Los Angeles. The effectiveness of the Student Zones program is measured twice a year through surveys administered to participants and homework helpers alike. More than 28,200 homework help sessions occurred in 2015/16. Eighty-six percent of students surveyed said the program helped them improve their grades. Student Zone helpers reported that their communication, organizational, and customer service skills improved as a result of helping kids do their homework.

**PROGRAM**
Homework Help
Tutoring

**LIBRARY**
Mission Viejo Library
Mission Viejo, California

**CONTACT PERSON**
Sarah Stimson, Library Manager, Public Services
949-830–7100 ext. 5132
sstimson@cityofmissionviejo.org

**PROGRAM WEB PAGE**
http://cityofmissionviejo.org/departments/library/library-services/homework-help-tutoring

**HOURS**
Homework Help is available to younger children during two hour-long sessions, Wednesday, 3:30 to 4:30 PM and 4:30 to 5:30 PM. Math and science tutoring for older students is scheduled in two shifts, Monday through Thursday, 6:30 to 7:30 PM and 7:30 to 8:30 PM.

**FUNDING SOURCE**
The program is part of the library's regular budget.

**STAFFING**
Both programs are staffed by high-level volunteers, who tend to be either part-time or retired teachers.

**TARGET POPULATION**
Homework Help is aimed at second- through sixth-grade students, while the tutoring program is for seventh through twelfth graders.

**PURPOSE**
The program's purpose is to help students succeed in school.

**SPECIAL FEATURES**
The single-outlet Mission Viejo Library serves an upper-middle-class planned community at the south end of Orange County. Homework Help, which used to be offered for an hour-and-a-half, was recently expanded to two hour-long sessions to give more children a chance to receive assistance. Each session accommodates up to eight kids. Parents can reserve a spot for their youngsters up to a week in advance and must sign a permission slip that explains the parameters of the program. Students are advised to come equipped with their questions, textbook, pencil and paper, and any other necessary materials.

The tutoring program, on the other hand, is offered to older students over two hour-long shifts, four nights a week. Subjects include pre-algebra, algebra I and II, geometry, trigonometry, pre-calculus, calculus, and physics. Different topics are covered each night depending on the tutor. A detailed schedule of subjects and tutors is posted on the program's web page. Each session accommodates up to six students, who are asked to attend no more than one session a week. Like Homework Help, a tutoring spot must be reserved in advance and requires parental permission. Tutoring sessions focus on completing specific homework assignments, working through study guides, and textbook lessons. Both Homework Help and the tutoring program are extremely popular and are limited only by the lack of available meeting space in the library.

---

**PROGRAM**
Library Study Center

**LIBRARY**
Paso Robles Public Library
Paso Robles, California

**CONTACT PERSON**
Melissa Bailey, Youth Services Librarian
805-237-3870
MBailey@prcity.com

**PROGRAM WEB PAGE**
www.prcity.com/government/departments/library/study-center.asp

**HOURS**
During the school year: Monday, Tuesday, Thursday, 2:30 to 4:40 PM, and Wednesday, 1:30 to 3:30 PM.
During summer: Monday through Thursday, 1:00 to 3:00 PM.

**FUNDING SOURCE**
The program is part of the library's regular budget. On a project-by-project basis, additional funds may be provided by the Friends of the Library or the Paso Robles Library Foundation.

**STAFFING**
The library's youth services librarian manages the Library Study Center. Other center staff include staff assistants III and staff assistants II as well as volunteers. Two adults are always present to oversee Study Center activities.

**TARGET POPULATION**
The program is aimed at kindergarteners through fifth graders, but is used mostly by third- and fourth-grade students from the dual-language immersion elementary school across the street.

**PURPOSE**
The program's purpose is to help students with homework, research, and reports.

## SPECIAL FEATURES

The program started as a corollary service offered in 1999 at the local Youth Arts facility. It eventually became a full-fledged library program when it moved to its own building in 2010. It is currently located in a modular unit which is part of a complex that also houses the California State Preschool and First 5 day care. The Study Center is open four afternoons a week. Children come over from the elementary school across the street as soon as classes end. The Study Center's first half-hour is designated as "quiet time," when students do homework either in groups or independently. Once their homework is completed, the kids are then allowed to use the Study Center's computers or play educational games. The facility is zoned as a classroom and so can only accommodate up to thirty-eight people at any one time.

The Library Study Center offers a lively, cheerful, and welcoming place to go after school. Most of the children come from low-income families and live in nearby housing projects. Backpacks are hung on hooks or piled under a sign that says "BACKPACKS HERE" by the front door. Students work at tables or on comfortable sofas. Everyone obviously enjoys being there. A small collection of books in English and Spanish fills one corner of the room. Homework completion is rewarded with a token, which the child can save or trade in, once a week, for a piece of candy, school supplies, or a trip to the "treasure box." The better the item, the more tokens required to trade. This system not only rewards the kids for doing their work, it also teaches responsibility and the benefits of being patient. The program is drop-in only, but most users visit daily.

---

## PROGRAM
Homework Centers

## LIBRARY
Saint Paul Public Library
Saint Paul, Minnesota

## CONTACT PERSON
Eric Whalen, Homework Center Coordinator
651-266-7433
eric.whalen@ci.stpaul.mn.us

## PROGRAM WEB PAGE
www.sppl.org/homework

## HOURS
Weekdays, 4:00 to 7:00 PM, exact days vary by branch. Sunday, 1:00 to 4:00 PM at three branches.

## FUNDING SOURCE
The program is part of the library's regular budget, though the Friends of the Library also provide funds for school supplies. The Homework Center periodically applies for grants to pay helpers to continue the service throughout the summer.

## STAFFING

The program is managed by a full-time library staff member, who works closely with the library's volunteer coordinator. A branch staff member is responsible for overseeing the program at each homework center site. Volunteers, work-study students, and service learners provide the homework assistance.

## TARGET POPULATION

Although students of all ages are welcome, third through fifth graders are the heaviest users of the program. About 25 percent of participants are adult learners.

## PURPOSE

The program's purpose is to advance student success in school and life through academic skill-building.

## SPECIAL FEATURES

Originated by AmeriCorps VISTA (Volunteers in Service to America), the library's homework help program was launched in 2003 to meet public demand. Eventually the Homework Centers became part of the library's regular service. Student achievement and after-school programs are a citywide priority, so the homework centers are but one of many such enterprises offered throughout Saint Paul. The Amherst H. Wilder Foundation, a nonprofit social services organization, tracks after-school activities citywide and provides a database of demographic and homework help usage to the library. Even though the library's homework program is drop-in only, students must check into the database every time they visit the homework center. Once registered, they write their names on a whiteboard and wait for the next available homework helper. Many helpers have specific areas of expertise, and so the site coordinator strategically pairs students and helpers according to subject. Sessions are conducted one-on-one, as much as possible, and typically last about thirty minutes each, though students can sign up for a second or third session if they need more help.

Many parents come to the Homework Center with their children—some are very involved in the session, some are not. Homework Center staff are trained to make the homework experience as positive as possible, but sometimes extra support is necessary to ensure that parents and other students are not a distraction. For students who need extra assistance, the library subscribes to Brainfuse's HelpNow online tutoring, which the library calls "Homework Rescue."

---

**PROGRAM**
Homework Help

**LIBRARY**
Seattle Public Library, Seattle, Washington

**CONTACT PERSON**
Josie Watanabe, Formal Learning Librarian
206-920-8154
Josie.Watanabe@spl.org

## PROGRAM WEB PAGE

www.spl.org/using-the-library/get-help/homework-help

## HOURS

Monday through Thursday, 4:30 to 7:30 PM

## FUNDING SOURCE

Seattle Public Library Foundation

## STAFFING

The formal learning librarian oversees the program systemwide, but a librarian-level homework center liaison is responsible for monitoring service at each site. Homework assistance is provided by volunteers.

## TARGET POPULATION

The program is aimed at kindergarteners through twelfth graders. Only 10 percent of participants systemwide come from homes where English is spoken.

## PURPOSE

The program's purpose is to provide a friendly, supportive learning environment for students of all ages.

## SPECIAL FEATURES

Offered in ten branches, this is a highly organized program that demonstrates the value of having a full-time coordinator who is also liaison to the citywide school district. Although academic success is one of the Seattle Public Library's service priorities, all requests for new branch homework centers are carefully considered before committing limited resources. The library tries not to duplicate community efforts and so works closely with the school district to decide where the program would be most effective. In the branches that do offer homework help, academic assistance is provided by a team of some 230 volunteers, 90 percent of whom are adults with at least one year of college. Homework helpers are expected to serve the entire school year. Individual volunteers are extremely popular, even though they rotate throughout the week. Eighty percent of the homework helpers continue from year to year.

The busiest homework help site is the Lake City branch, where the teen services librarian personally greets every student and volunteer by name. Not only do young people get excellent assistance with their assignments, they are also eligible to receive a free meal from the Hunger Intervention Program, which brings food to the library every day the homework center is open. At 5:30 PM, staff announce over the branch's loudspeaker that meals are available in the lobby for the next hour. Children help themselves and eat away from the rest of the library. At the end of the school year, the teen services librarian hosts a pizza party for the homework volunteers as well as all students who participated in the program. Certificates of achievement are ceremoniously awarded to the kids to encourage them to return again in the fall.

**PROGRAM**
SUCCESS

**LIBRARY**
Winters Branch, Yolo County
Winters, California

**CONTACT PERSON**
Toni Mendieta, Winters Community Library Supervisor
530-795-9127
tony.mendieta@yolocounty.org

**PROGRAM WEB PAGE**
www.yolocounty.org/Home/Components/Calendar/Event/35148/2595?selcat=81

**HOURS**
Monday, Tuesday, and Thursday, 3:30 to 5:00 PM

**FUNDING SOURCE**
RISE, Inc. (Rural Innovations in Social Economics), a social services agency that receives state funding for local projects.

**STAFFING**
A RISE employee oversees the SUCCESS program at the library as part of her full-time job duties in the community. Homework help is provided by high school students, called mentors.

**TARGET POPULATION**
The program is aimed at first through eighth graders, primarily from low-income families.

**PURPOSE**
Students receive help with homework and reading from high school mentors.

**SPECIAL FEATURES**
Although held in the library's community room three afternoons a week, the SUCCESS program is imported from a social services agency, called RISE, Inc., that provides educational and other activities to low-income families in the community. Homework assistance is provided to elementary and middle school kids by high school mentors, who are required to complete community service. One mentor, who has been with the program since eighth grade, said he enjoys "giving back" to the community and is now thinking of pursuing a career in political science as a result of "having his mind opened to kids' needs." The younger students work on school assignments for forty-five minutes or read with their mentor. The rest of the session is spent completing educational worksheets or engaging in team-building activities. Every week, either a library staff member or the local high school librarian conducts a fifteen-minute book talk. In addition, the branch librarian engages the students and their mentors in a monthly Community World Café conversation, which sometimes leads to critical thinking expressed through art and poetry.

Parents attend a required orientation before registering their children into the program for the entire year, including summer. They must then sign permission and photo release forms and give medical treatment consent. The program is capped at thirty-five students. Since there is always a waiting list, kids are allowed only three unexcused absences before being dropped from the program. At the beginning of the school year, the SUCCESS coordinator works with the children to develop rules of behavior, which she calls "agreements." These are all phrased in positive terms and do not use words like "don't" or "no." Good learning behavior is rewarded through outings, like camping trips and visits to the local skateboard park.

# Community Assessment Tools

## ✓ PARENT SURVEY

1. What grade levels are your child(ren) currently enrolled in?

   6    7    8    9    10    11    12

2. In what subject areas do your children need help or tutoring? (Please indicate specific subjects)

   a. Math: _____

   b. Science: _____

   c. Foreign Language: _____

   d. History: _____

   e. Literature: _____

   f. Other: _____

3. What type of homework do you notice your children being assigned?

   a. Essays _____

   b. Research Projects _____

   c. Homework from the Textbook _____

   d. Science Fair Projects _____

   e. Other _____

4. What types of resources would be helpful to your child(ren) in a homework center?

   a. Reference materials, such as dictionaries or encyclopedias

   b. Tutors

   c. Textbooks or Teacher's Guides for the textbook

   d. Computers

   e. Other _____

Source: Sian Brannon and WyLaina Hildreth. 2011. "Teen Homework Centers—Minimum Resources for Most Budgets." *Texas Library Journal* 87 (Spring): 19–25.

## ✅ STUDENT SURVEY

1. What grade are you in?

   6      7      8      9      10      11      12

2. In what subject areas do you need help or tutoring? (Please indicate specific subjects)

   a. Math: _____

   b. Science: _____

   c. Foreign Language: _____

   d. History: _____

   e. Literature: _____

   f. Other: _____

3. What type of homework are your teachers giving you to do?

   a. Essays

   b. Research Projects

   c. Homework from the Textbook

   d. Science Fair Projects

   e. Other _____

4. If the library had a homework center, what types of resources would help you complete your homework?

   a. Reference materials, such as dictionaries or encyclopedias

   b. Tutors

   c. Textbooks or Teacher's Guides for the textbook

   d. Computers

   e. Other _____

Source: Sian Brannon and WyLaina Hildreth. 2011. "Teen Homework Centers—Minimum Resources for Most Budgets." *Texas Library Journal* 87 (Spring): 19–25.

## ❷ TEACHER SURVEY

1. What grade levels do you currently teach?

     6    7    8    9    10    11    12

2. What subject areas do you teach? (Please indicate specific subjects)

   a. Math: _____

   b. Science: _____

   c. Foreign Language: _____

   d. History: _____

   e. Literature: _____

   f. Other: _____

3. What type of homework do you normally assign?

   a. I don't assign homework

   b. Essays

   c. Research Projects

   d. Homework from the Textbook

   e. Science Fair Projects

   f. Other _____

4. What types of resources would be helpful to your students in a homework center?

   a. Reference materials, such as dictionaries or encyclopedias

   b. Books on the subjects I teach

   c. Databases

   d. Tutors

   e. Textbooks or Teacher's Guides for the textbook

   f. Computers

   g. Other _____

Source: Sian Brannon and WyLaina Hildreth. 2011. "Teen Homework Centers—Minimum Resources for Most Budgets." *Texas Library Journal* 87 (Spring): 19–25.

# Homework Staff Recruitment Announcements

**Homework Help Lead Tutor positions available**

Hennepin County Library is seeking two enthusiastic and creative tutors, passionate about serving youth and families, to manage the delivery of the K-12 Homework Help afterschool tutoring service at **Hennepin County Library – North Regional** and **Hennepin County Library - Brookdale**. The goals of this program are to help children and young people master academic concepts, and to complete homework assignments. Lead Tutors are responsible for providing academic and social support to students, overseeing the day-to-day program activities and space, supporting volunteer tutors, and providing some direct tutoring service.

Lead Tutors work approximately 15 hours per week September through May, and are paid an hourly rate of $17.84.

The primary duties and responsibilities of this position include:

- Set up for, start and end program at publicized times.
- Ensure that the Homework Help program flows smoothly.
- Provide orientation, support, and some training to volunteer tutors.
- Assist in promoting the Homework Help program and in recruiting community volunteers.
- Provide tutoring services to children and teens in grades K-12
- Collect and report program data (ex: monthly attendance numbers, administer student surveys)
- Become familiar with and promote library resources to students, families, and volunteers
- Attend required meetings and training sessions

Minimum Qualifications:
- Must be able to work during program hours.
- Must have some post-secondary education, with strong knowledge in literacy and mathematical concepts.
- Must have basic computer skills, including the ability to navigate online systems and email.

If you have questions about the positions, please contact Katherine Debertin, Youth Programs & Services Manager, by email at kdebertin@hclib.org or by phone at 612-543-8032.

To apply, please submit your resume and cover letter to Katherine Debertin, kdebertin@hclib.org by July 15, 2016.

2016-2017

Source: Hennepin County Library

## BELLE COOLEDGE LIBRARY TEEN COACH APPLICATION

**Dear Prospective HOMEWORK COACH:**
We are delighted that you are interested in joining the Belle Cooledge Homework Zone as a COACH. In order to give your application full consideration, please read and carefully follow the instructions on this form. Return the completed application and the required forms to the program contact at your high school or to the service desk at the Belle Cooledge Library.

**About the Program**
As a coach, you will work with a student or a small group of elementary or middle school students. The Homework Zone is held Thursdays, 3:30 to 5:00 pm, from October 2014 to May 2015.

Training will be provided in the form of an orientation and may include occasional workshops that are designed to present information specific to the coaching process. The orientation will also provide a forum for coaches to share their experiences and ideas. The orientation provides a foundation for your work as a coach; however, an important part of your training will be "on-the-job," as you learn from your interactions with students.

Benefits of participation include building a college or employment résumé, receiving class or community service credit, learning new skills, meeting other teens in the program, having fun, and most importantly, contributing to the success of the youngsters you coach!

**Eligibility**
To become a Homework Zone coach, you must (1) meet the program eligibility guidelines which are listed below and (2) attend the orientation.

In addition to having a solid academic background, personal qualities are very important. These include patience, ingenuity, and the ability to engage in a meaningful way with youngsters. Our students come from a variety of ethnic, linguistic, and socio-economic backgrounds, therefore, your ability to relate and collaborate in a positive manner is critically important. Previous experience in educational settings is valued, but not required. Eligibility requirements include:

- Currently enrolled in high school (10th through 12th grades)
- Completed application submitted with a copy of your most recent report card
- Recommendation from at least one teacher
- Overall 3.0 GPA
- Ability to speak and understand English well enough to communicate clearly

FORM Application for TEEN COACHES October 2014 June 2015

Source: Sacramento Public Library

**Selection Process**

All applications will be reviewed by the program core team and Program Coordinator. Each applicant will be evaluated on her/his responses on the application form and academic standing (as evidenced by the report card and teacher recommendation). Coaches will be notified of their acceptance and informed about next steps that will include attending the orientation.

**Coaches' Responsibilities**

If you are accepted into the program, you will be expected to:

- Attend orientation, training sessions, and all scheduled meetings
- Be on time and be prepared for meeting with students
- Complete all records and forms required by the program and submit on time
- Communicate with the Homework Zone Program Coordinator about planned or unplanned absences, late arrivals or other issues
- Become familiar with the resources available at the Belle Cooledge Library
- Be committed to being a partner in the process of helping students achieve academic goals
- Maintain confidentiality regarding each student's information (personal and academic)
- Assist students with homework, projects, test preparation, and other subject-related issues
- Set a good example and be a role model for students to emulate.

*PLEASE RETAIN THIS PAGE FOR YOUR REFERENCE*

FORM Application for TEEN COACHES October 2014 June 2015

# Homework Helper Application Forms

**Prospect Heights Public Library**
**Study Buddy Homework Center**
**High School Volunteer Application**
**2013-2014 School Year**

Tuesdays 6:00-8:00 pm
October 1, 8, 15, 22 and 29
November 5, 12 and 19
December 3, 10 and 17
January 28
February 4, 11 and 18
March 4 and 11

**Volunteers**
Are The HEART Of
The LIBRARY!

*********************************************************************************

Study Buddy Homework Center meets on Tuesday evenings from 6:00 to 8:00 pm during the school year on assigned dates. Study Buddies are high school volunteers who tutor elementary school children with their homework.

As a volunteer at Prospect Heights Public Library District, I commit myself to the "Study Buddy Homework Center" for two hours per week when available.

I agree to:
    Attend orientation and training when necessary.
    Accept guidance from the Library staff.
    Notify the Youth Services Librarian by phone/email of an absence as far in advance as possible.
    Comply with Library policies.
The Library agrees to:
    Provide a pleasant work environment.
    Provide training when necessary.
    Appreciate the commitment and task accomplished.

Name: _____

Address: _____ City: _____ Zip: _____

Cell Phone: _____ Home Phone: _____

Email Address: _____

School: _____ Grade: _____

Signature: _____ Date: _____

Parent Signature: _____ Date: _____

**Thank You and Welcome!**
**Alice Johnson Bisanz, Youth Services School Liaison, Library Volunteer Coordinator**
**847-259-9150, Ext. 31 - Fax: 847-259-4602 - ajbisanz@phpl.info**

**Prospect Heights Public Library District**
12 North Elm Street, Prospect Heights, IL 60070
www.phpl.info • 847-259-3500

Source: Prospect Heights Public Library

**BELLE COOLEDGE LIBRARY HOMEWORK ZONE COACH INFORMATION**

Feel free to attach additional pages as necessary. The completed application should be returned to the program team member at your school or to the service desk at the Belle Cooledge Library **by September 30, 2014**. *Be sure to attach a copy of your most recent report card.*

Name: _____
                  First                                                  Last

Address: _____

Home phone: _____  Cell phone: _____

Email: _____

❑ I am over 13 years of age        ❑ Male ❑ Female

Grade:  ❑ Sophomore  ❑ Junior  ❑ Senior

Name of School:_____

Have you previously participated in another tutoring/mentoring program?
❑ No ❑ Yes

If yes, where and when? _____

Do you speak a language other than English fluently?   ❑ No   ❑ Yes

If yes, what language? _____

Are you willing to mentor your student in that language?   ❑ No   ❑ Yes

Are you willing to work with students whose second language is English?      ❑ No   ❑ Yes

How did you hear about the Homework Zone Program?
        ❑  Recruited by a student at my school
        ❑  School Club
        ❑  Flyer in the library
        ❑  Sacramento Public Library web site

Are there any subject areas you do **NOT** want to coach?

_____

FORM Application for TEEN COACHES October 2014 June 2015

Source: Sacramento Public Library

**Agreements (please check each item after reading, sign and date)**

Information on this form will be used for program purposes only.

❏ I understand that the Belle Cooledge Library reserves the right to screen volunteer coaches and may not accept me into the program.

❏ I understand that I have an obligation to maintain confidentiality.

❏ I will be able to attend the mandatory coach orientation on Thursday, October 2 at 3:30 pm.

❏ I understand that the Homework Zone is held on Thursdays from 3:30 to 5 pm.

❏ I understand that my volunteer work is a commitment and when I cannot work on the assigned date and time, I will notify the Homework Zone Program Coordinator.

❏ I understand that I will not be paid for my services as a volunteer coach and that I am giving my time freely to the library.

_____          Date

Teen Applicant's Signature

I understand and support the responsibilities stated herein. I give my permission for my child to participate in the Homework Zone Program.

_____          Date

Parent or Legal Guardian's Signature

## EMERGENCY CONTACT INFORMATION

**EMERGENCY CONTACT #1**

_____

Parent or Guardian's Name

_____

Email Address

_____

Home Phone Number

_____

Cell Phone Number

**EMERGENCY CONTACT #2**

_____

Name and relationship to student

_____

Email Address

_____

Home Phone Number

_____

Cell Phone Number

## PLEASE COMPLETE, SIGN, AND RETURN THIS FORM

FORM Application for TEEN COACHES October 2014 June 2015

*Homework Zone*
BROUGHT TO YOU BY SACRAMENTO PUBLIC LIBRARY

**Applicant's Name:**_____

| TEACHER RECOMMENDATION |
| --- |

I, _____recommend _____
          Teacher's Name                                          Student's Name

for the position of Coach in the Homework Zone Program at the Belle Cooledge Library for the following reasons:

_____

_____

_____

_____

_____

_____

_____

_____

Teacher's Signature                                          Date

FORM Application for TEEN COACHES October 2014 June 2015

# Homework Helper Contract

**Volunteer** ●●●●●● **KCLS Volunteer Agreement** ◇Study Zone◇

**Note: This Agreement is required of all KCLS volunteers, regardless of assignment.**

I, _____ (please print volunteer's name clearly)
hereby agree to volunteer my services to King County Library System (KCLS) as a
__Study Zone Tutor__ (I understand that this is uncompensated volunteer service. No offer of
regular employment is sought or implied. I agree to volunteer with KCLS in the following
capacity:

Tutors assist elementary through high school aged students (grades K- 12) with their homework. Study Zone
tutors assist with all subjects for grades K-8. Each tutor specializes in the advanced topic(s) of their choice
when assisting with high school level subjects. Each tutor works with students in a group setting of typically
1-5 students.

I agree to volunteer according to the following schedule:

*Library or Substitute area:* _____     *Day / Time* _____

The minimum Study Zone volunteer commitment is 2 hours per week for Library Tutors and 3 hours per week
for SZ Online Tutors, for the duration of the current semester. Study Zone tutors may renew their commitment
at the start of each semester, September-January, February-June, *July-August (summer session is optional).*

I understand that either I or KCLS can end my volunteer service at any time.

I agree to participate in KCLS volunteer orientation and/or training. Staff will provide orientation to the
library, the staff workroom, break areas, and a place for my personal items while scheduled.

I agree to wear KCLS volunteer identification (lanyard and badge) while volunteering.

I acknowledge that, although serving as a volunteer, the public may regard me as a representative of
KCLS, and thus I will dress and conduct myself accordingly. I will be courteous and helpful to patrons
and other staff members and I will not engage in the unacceptable behaviors listed at the end of this
Agreement.

I agree to contact my Volunteer Supervisor or other library staff as soon as possible if I unexpectedly
cannot fulfill a scheduled volunteer commitment. Failure to **notify** staff that I cannot fulfill a scheduled
assignment, may lead KLCS to end my volunteer service.

I understand that KCLS has comprehensive general liability coverage limited to coverage for volunteers
working within the scope of their assignment and on behalf of KCLS. I will report any on-the-job injury
or illness, no matter how minor, to my Volunteer Supervisor and/or to a KCLS manager.

I will abide by KCLS policy and will not:
• Reveal any KCLS confidential information, including patron information.
• Use the patron database (Integrated Library System).
• Handle Library System money.
• Perform library work off KCLS property, except as described in "virtual" volunteer assignments and
  specific offsite volunteer assignments.
• Work without direct supervision until I have cleared all required background checks.
  *Note: volunteers under age 14 will have staff supervision.*

My signature, below, indicates that I have read the above statements and a KCLS staff member has
satisfactorily answered my questions about them.

This agreement will be in effect for the duration of my volunteer services, beginning this date:

_____

KCLS Staff: Please return completed Study Zone Volunteer Agreements to "Annie Poyner - Study Zone, Service Center"

Source: King County Library System

**Unacceptable Behaviors Enumerated.** The following practices are examples of unacceptable conduct that may lead to ending your volunteer service.

a. Destruction, damage, avoidable wastage, theft or unauthorized use of property that is not the property of the volunteer.
b. Reporting for my assignment while under any influence of alcohol, narcotics or other controlled substances.
c. Possession of alcohol, narcotics, controlled substances or weapons on KCLS premises.
d. Failure to observe safety practices, rules, regulations and instructions.
e. Failure to promptly report to your assignment supervisor or to another KCLS staff member any injury or accident sustained while fulfilling your volunteer assignment
f. Negligence that results in injury to others.
g. Misrepresenting yourself as speaking for the King County Library System and making statements or taking other actions that are intended to or could reasonably be expected to damage the integrity or reputation of the Library.
h. Sexual, racial or other unlawful harassment or discrimination toward another volunteer, staff member or member of the public.
i. Engaging patrons, volunteers or employees in religious instruction, proselytizing, or worship while working with them during a volunteer assignment.
j. Acting in a manner inconsistent with common sense standards of conduct necessary to the welfare of the King County Library System, its staff members and the general public we serve.
k. Acting in any manner inconsistent with good customer services practices in interactions with patrons or others.

## STUDY ZONE VOLUNTEER GUIDELINES

1. All contact between volunteers and children/young people must take place in the library.
2. Volunteers should be aware of the child's natural dignity and sense of self. Children are now often taught by parents and teachers not to allow non-family members to touch them; please respect this and do not initiate close contact.
3. Any problems with children or parents should be referred to the library staff so s/he can resolve them.
4. Volunteers may not offer to drive or walk children/young people anywhere outside the library.
5. Volunteers should not initiate discussions of ethnic, religious, political or sexual matters with any of the children/young people.
6. Volunteers should show all non-library material to the library staff before using them or presenting them to the children.
7. Volunteers and students can bring their own personal beverages or snack to the library. However, due to the prevalence of food allergies and dietary restrictions, volunteers and staff cannot provide food or drinks to the students.
8. Volunteers should be on time as scheduled and call the library if they will not be able to work. Whenever possible volunteers should make arrangements for a substitute tutor to fill in for their absence.
9. Volunteers who intend to discontinue participation in the program should promptly notify the *Study Zone* coordinator and library staff. Please provide a minimum of two weeks advance notice.
10. Volunteers should consult with their individual library staff for specific rules regarding that library.

Applicant Signature _____

Print Name _____ Date _____

## STUDY ZONE SUBSTITUTE LOCATIONS

I am willing to substitute for other Study Zone tutors at these libraries:

| | | | | | |
|---|---|---|---|---|---|
| | | | ☐ Algona-Pacific | ☐ Auburn | |
| ☐ Bellevue | ☐ Black Diamond | ☐ Bothell | ☐ Boulevard Park | ☐ Burien | ☐ Carnation |
| ☐ Covington | ☐ Des Moines | ☐ Duvall | ☐ Fairwood | ☐ Fall City | ☐ Federal Way |
| ☐ Federal Way 320th | ☐ Foster | ☐ Issaquah | ☐ Kenmore | ☐ Kent | ☐ Kingsgate |
| ☐ Kirkland | ☐ Lake Forest Park | ☐ Lake Hills | ☐ Maple Valley | ☐ Mercer Island | ☐ Muckleshoot |
| ☐ Newport Way | ☐ North Bend | ☐ Redmond | ☐ Renton | ☐ Renton Highlands | ☐ Richmond Beach |
| ☐ Sammamish | ☐ Shoreline | ☐ Skykomish | ☐ Skyway | ☐ Snoqualmie | ☐ Valley View |
| ☐ Vashon Island | ☐ White Center | ☐ Woodinville | ☐ Woodmont | | |

KCLS Staff: Please return completed Study Zone Volunteer Agreements to "Annie Poyner - Study Zone. Service Center"

# Homework Staff Job Descriptions

 **Boston Public Library**
**Homework Help**
**Mentor Job Description**

BPL Homework Help mentors are high-achieving teens who fill a variety of roles in the library. Mentors are valued by librarians, children, parents, and the community for the difference they make in children's lives.

## Expectations

- **Good grades:** Maintain a 3.0 GPA (grade point average) or above in school. Report cards may be requested at any point in your employment to confirm this expectation is being met.
- **Timeliness and reliability:** Arrive on time and stay to the end of your shift. If you are going to be absent, you must contact a librarian at your assigned branch. Missing more than 2 shifts per pay period is grounds for dismissal.
- **Patience and adaptability:** Be friendly, approachable and flexible. Every shift will be a little bit different and it is important that you can adjust to different children, situations, and duties, as outlined in this description.
- **Conduct:** As a role model in the library, you will be expected to behave appropriately, including following all library rules and policies.
- **Communication:** Check your email regularly for messages from the homework help manager and your branch's children's librarian. Always exchange contact information with the librarians at your assigned branch so they can reach you and you can reach them when necessary.
- **Training:** Attend orientation and 3 scheduled trainings run by Harvard University. You will be paid for these meetings.

## Roles and Responsibilities, in order of importance

- **Homework help**
  To the best of your ability, you will help children in grades K-8 to understand concepts in all subjects and be able to display that understanding through their homework. The library's resources – books, databases, public computers, librarians – are all available to you to complete these duties.
- **Mentorship**
  Children come to the library for academic reasons but also to have fun and hang out. It is within your duties to make their library experience a positive one. This could mean playing board games, reading aloud, drawing, assisting with craft projects, or just talking. Share your unique interests and ask the librarian if you need special supplies, access to a computer, etc.
- **Statistics Collection**
  You will keep relevant statistics on the activities you do when mentoring and tutoring students as part of the Homework Help program.
- **Library program assistance**

| Boston Public Library | Mentor Application | page **1** of **2** |
|---|---|---|

Source: Boston Public Library

You may be called upon to attend or assist with afterschool library programs if you are not busy with the above duties. These programs can be an important point of mentorship, encouraging children to get involved in library activities. Programs will be run mainly by librarians or professionals hired to deliver these programs; you will only be assisting and only during the time you are being paid to work. You are not required to stay past your scheduled work time to complete these duties. You will not be paid extra if you exceed your work time.

- **Other duties as assigned by the librarian**
  The children's librarian at your branch may request your help with any number of tasks to support the environment and programs at the library. These duties cannot require you to exceed your scheduled shift and must be in the children's and/or teen room.

**Benefits**

- Earn $10 per hour. Pay checks are mailed 5 times during the year.
- Attend paid trainings on relevant topics and skills. Trainings are led by the Harvard University's Teaching and Learning Partnerships team and may offer opportunities for leadership within the program.
- An end-of-year bowling party to celebrate your contributions during the school year.
- Enhance your résumé and gain references for college and future jobs. Recommendation letters may be provided by request to those whose performance recommends them.
- Be an essential part of your community, making the library a safe and fun place for children to spend time.

HOMEWORK CENTER COORDINATOR (SEASONAL)     PD536-8/16     Page 1

## CUYAHOGA COUNTY PUBLIC LIBRARY

### Position Description

| Title:  Homework Center Coordinator (Seasonal) | PD536 | Grade: Off-Scale |
|---|---|---|
| Supervisor's Title:  Library Manager or Designee (with oversight from the Youth Services Manager/Designee) | | FLSA: NE |
| Positions Supervised:  Homework Center Volunteers and America Reads Tutors | | |

### GENERAL SUMMARY

Under moderate supervision, oversees the operations of the Homework Center, including supervising tutors and volunteers, and assisting individuals or groups of students with homework activities. Prepares analyses and reports on center usage. Researches and implements new services.

This position is part-time and operates seasonally from September through May with work breaks that coincide with partner universities.  Operates part-time at 10 to 14 hours per week, 2.5 hours daily that begins no earlier than 3:30 p.m., Monday through Thursday. (Hours may vary during start-up and take-down of the Homework Center.)  In cooperation and consultation with Branch Manager or designee, the Homework Center Coordinator facilitates and assures the smooth operation of the Homework Center.  The Youth Services Manager or designee, in consort with branch supervision, oversees each Homework Center site to guarantee quality and consistency of service.  This position may be extended to cover summer or alternate programming on a case by case basis.

### JOB REQUIREMENTS

Competencies that an incumbent should be able to demonstrate and that are reflected in the knowledge, skills and abilities that lead to satisfactory accomplishment of the Essential Job Functions, include the competency dimensions of Communications Skills, Empathy, Feedback, Listening, Coaching, Persistence/Perseverance, Problem Solving Ability, Customer Service, Perception/Judgment, Results Focus, Time Management, Attention to Detail, Dependability, Diversity Focus, and Planning & Organizing.  In addition, incumbents are expected to demonstrate proficiency in the Function/Task Specific dimension of Computer Knowledge and Use.

*Specific Knowledge, Skills, and Abilities required include:*

1.  Proficiency in English grammar, spelling, punctuation, and simple mathematical functions such as addition, subtraction, multiplication, division, percentages, ratios, etc.

2.  Skill in assigning, prioritizing, monitoring, and reviewing work assignments.

3.  Skill in mentoring and training employees with varying educational backgrounds

HOMEWORK CENTER COORDINATOR (SEASONAL)     PD536-8/16     Page 2

and aptitudes.

4.    Excellent organizational, problem solving and analytical skills.

5.    Skill in providing high quality customer service, including assessing and resolving customer questions and needs while adhering to customer service guidelines and procedures.

6.    Basic skill in the use of personal computer software or systems applicable to the essential functions of the job, which may include any or all of the following: email/calendar software, internet/intranet browsers, word processing, spreadsheets, database software, and various systems or software used by CCPL.

7.    Ability to provide comprehensive customer service, including delivery of accurate, prompt, and courteous assistance, both orally and in writing, to adults and children.

8.    Ability to use Library resources effectively and efficiently.

## ESSENTIAL JOB FUNCTIONS

1.    Complies with Cuyahoga County Public Library's policies, rules, guidelines, procedures, requirements, standards, and practices applicable to the job, including (but not limited to) work scheduling and attendance, customer service, use of Library property, computer use, personal conduct, and confidentiality.

2.    Responsible for recruitment and training, in cooperation with Library staff, of Homework Center volunteers.

3.    Provides daily supervision for America Reads tutors; verifies and sends time records to America Reads Coordinator.

4.    Directs activities of the Homework Center.  Determines student needs and appropriate activity.  Coaches volunteers and tutors.  Helps volunteers deal with challenging students.

5.    Maintains student registration and usage statistics.

6.    Provides monthly and annual reports for library management on Center highlights, statistics, research study and concerns.

7.    Orders supplies for Homework Center as needed.

8.    Is liaison between Homework Center, branch supervision and Youth Services.

9.    May contact teachers and schools to publicize Homework Center programs and request information on school assignment.

10. Provision of snacks to participants provided in partnership by the Cleveland

HOMEWORK CENTER COORDINATOR (SEASONAL)     PD536-8/16     Page 3

Foodbank.

The intent of this position description is to provide a representative summary of the major duties and responsibilities performed by incumbents of this job. Incumbents may be requested to perform job-related tasks other than those specifically presented in this description.

*Summary Minimum Education & Experience Required*

1.  Bachelors Degree or equivalent (e.g. combination of some college plus work experience as teacher's aide).  Teacher Certification strongly preferred.

2.  Minimum one year direct experience working with children Grades K-10 in an educational setting.

## OTHER TESTING/LICENSES REQUIRED

1.  A criminal background check is required.

2.  A pre-employment screening for drug and nicotine usage is required.

## PHYSICAL DEMANDS AND WORKING CONDITIONS

1.  Position is physically comfortable, individual is normally seated and has discretion about walking, standing, etc.  Occasionally lifts lightweight objects.  Some use of computer terminal.

2.  Position is seasonal as described in the General Summary

## CUYAHOGA COUNTY PUBLIC LIBRARY

### Position Description

| Title: Homework Mentor (Seasonal- Part Time) | LLD PD571 | Grade: Off-Scale |
|---|---|---|
| Supervisor's Title: Public Services Librarian- Children's | | FLSA: NE |
| Positions Supervised: N/a | | |

### GENERAL SUMMARY

Under moderate supervision, assists individuals or groups of students with homework activities. Prepares analyses and reports on homework/study services.

This position is part-time and operates seasonally from September through May with breaks that coincide with local school district. Operates part-time at 8 to 10 hours per week, approximately 2.5 hours daily, Monday through Thursday. (Hours vary according to local school district.) In cooperation and consultation with Public Services Librarian, the Homework Mentor facilitates and assures homework assistance to student library visitors. The Youth Programming Manager or designee, in consort with branch supervision, oversees homework services to guarantee quality and consistency of service. This position may be extended to cover summer or alternate programming on a case by case basis.

### JOB REQUIREMENTS

Competencies that an incumbent should be able to demonstrate and that are reflected in the knowledge, skills and abilities that lead to satisfactory accomplishment of the Essential Job Functions, include the competency dimensions of Communications Skills, Empathy, Feedback, Listening, Coaching, Persistence/Perseverance, Problem Solving Ability, Customer Service, Perception/Judgment, Results Focus, Time Management, Attention to Detail, Dependability, Diversity Focus, and Planning & Organizing. In addition, incumbents are expected to demonstrate proficiency in the Function/Task Specific dimension of Computer Knowledge and Use.

*Specific Knowledge, Skills, and Abilities required include:*

1. Proficiency in English grammar, spelling, punctuation, and simple mathematical functions such as addition, subtraction, multiplication, division, percentages, ratios, etc.

2. Skill in assigning, prioritizing, monitoring, and reviewing work assignments.

3. Skill in mentoring and working with volunteers with varying educational backgrounds and aptitudes.

4. Excellent organizational, problem solving and analytical skills.

HOMEWORK CENTER MENTOR     LLD PD571-03/16       Page 2
(SEASONAL/PART-TIME)

5.    Basic skill in the use of personal computer software or systems applicable to the essential functions of the job, which may include any or all of the following: email/calendar software, internet/intranet browsers, word processing, spreadsheets, database software, and various systems or software used by CCPL.

6.    Ability to provide comprehensive customer service, including delivery of accurate, prompt, and courteous assistance, both orally and in writing to adults and children.

7.    Ability to use Library resources effectively and efficiently.

## ESSENTIAL JOB FUNCTIONS

1.    Complies with Cuyahoga County Public Library's policies, rules, guidelines, procedures, requirements, standards, and practices applicable to the job, including (but not limited to) work scheduling and attendance, customer service, use of Library property, computer use, personal conduct, and confidentiality.

2.    Determines student homework needs and provides appropriate support.

3.    Provides monthly and annual reports for library management on homework services including but not limited to highlights, statistics, and concerns.

4.    Provision of snacks to participants provided in partnership by the Cleveland Foodbank.

The intent of this position description is to provide a representative summary of the major duties and responsibilities performed by incumbents of this job. Incumbents may be requested to perform job-related tasks other than those specifically presented in this description.

*Summary Minimum Education & Experience Required*

1.    Bachelors Degree or equivalent (e.g. combination of some college plus work experience as teacher's aide). Teacher Certification strongly preferred.

2.    Minimum one year direct experience working with children Grades K-12 in an educational setting.

## OTHER TESTING/LICENSES REQUIRED

1.    A criminal background check is required.

HOMEWORK CENTER MENTOR          LLD PD571-03/16                    Page 3
(SEASONAL/PART-TIME)

    2.    A pre-employment screening for drug and nicotine usage is required.

**PHYSICAL DEMANDS AND WORKING CONDITIONS**

    1.    No major sources of working conditions discomfort, i.e. standard work environment with possible minor inconveniences due to occasional noise, crowded working conditions, and/or minor heating, cooling or ventilation problems.

    2.    Position involves extensive walking throughout the interior of the Library.

# Assistant Management Analyst (Literacy Tutor/Learning Coordinator)

Class Code: 1132G

Bargaining Unit: PROFESSIONAL UNIT (MEA)

CITY OF SAN DIEGO
Established Date: Jul 28, 1995

**SALARY RANGE**
$21.38 - $25.99 Hourly
$1,710.40 - $2,079.20 Biweekly
$44,470.40 - $54,059.20 Annually

**JOB INFORMATION:**

Assistant Management Analyst (Literacy Tutor/Learner Coordinator) positions facilitate learner enrollment by conducting testing, assessment and counseling to determine program eligibility; coordinate matching of learners with volunteer tutors; monitor tutor/learner progress; interview, train, supervise, and evaluate volunteer staff; develop and coordinate volunteer assessment counselor training programs; maintain referral sources and other data to comply with reporting standards of program stakeholders; make presentations to community agencies, human services programs, local businesses and schools to promote San Diego Public Library programs; and perform other duties as assigned.

NOTE:
- The current vacancies are limited, hourly position in support of the Library's Do Your Homework @ the Library Program.

**TYPICAL REQUIREMENTS:**

You must meet the following requirements on the date you apply, unless otherwise indicated.

EDUCATION: Bachelor's Degree or equivalent education (i.e., minimum completed units = 120 semester/180 quarter).

NOTE:
- Additional qualifying experience may be substituted for education lacked on a year-for-year basis. One year of full-time experience = 30 semester/45 quarter college-level units.

EXPERIENCE: One year of full-time professional experience working in a literacy or adult basic education program.

NOTE:
- A Master's Degree in Education, Teaching, or a closely related field may be substituted for the required experience.

LICENSE: A valid California Class C Driver Licenseis required at the time of hire.

HIGHLY DESIRABLE:
- Supervisory or lead experience coordinating the work of volunteers or paid staff who provide adult literacy instruction and/or program support. A Master's Degree in Education or Teaching.
- A post-baccalaureate teaching credential.

REQUIRED DOCUMENTS (MUST SUBMIT WITH APPLICATION):
- Proof of degree/transcripts, if utilized to meet the minimum requirements.

Required documents should be attached electronically to your application. If you are unable to attach at the time of application submittal, you must submit them as soon as possible via fax: (619) 533-3337; or to the Employment Information Center: City of San Diego Personnel Department, 1200 Third Avenue - Suite 300, San Diego, CA 92101. Include your name and the title of the position for which you are applying.

**TYPICAL SCREENING PROCESS:**

Source: City of San Diego

The screening process will consist of a comprehensive evaluation of the application for applicable education, experience, and/or training to ensure all minimum requirements have been met. Successful candidates will be placed on a list which will be used to fill position vacancies during the next one year. For each vacancy, only those candidates with the most appropriate qualifications will be contacted by the hiring department for an interview.

**SUPPLEMENTAL INFORMATION:**
PRE-EMPLOYMENT REQUIREMENTS: Employment offers are conditional pending the results of all screening processes that are applicable to this job, which may include but are not limited to the following:  Confirmation of citizenship/legal right to work in the United States; completion of a pre-employment medical review/exam (which may include drug/alcohol testing); reference checks; and a fingerprint check.  The fingerprints will be submitted to the Federal Bureau of Investigation and/or the California Department of Justice for a conviction record report. Certain positions may require additional screening processes which may include a polygraph examination and/or background investigation.  All of these processes must be successfully completed before employment begins.  A positive test for alcohol, illegal drugs or inadequately explained prescription drugs, misrepresentation, falsification, or omission of pertinent facts in any step of the screening/selection process may be cause for disqualification and/or termination of employment.  Nothing in this job posting constitutes an expressed or implied contract for employment with the City of San Diego. Applicants must notify the Personnel Department of any changes in their name, address (home, email), or phone number or they may miss employment opportunities.

Assistant Management Analyst (Option Title: Literacy Tutor/Learner Coordinator)

**JOB CATEGORIES:**

Library

**TITLE CHANGES:**

## Tutoring Guidelines:
### Tutor Expectations

The tutor's goal is to provide direction and present study skills. **Tutors should not answer questions outright or do a student's homework for them.**

### Study Zone Tutors:

- Work with 1-5 students per tutor in a group setting
- Help with all subjects for grades K-6
- Specialize in one or more subjects at the high school level

*If you consistently get more than 5 students per tutor at each session, please update the Study Zone coordinator so that additional tutors can be assigned to your session.*

*You can update your advanced high school subjects and languages in your MyVolunteerPage.com on the My Profile tab under Additional Info.*

### Tutors are expected to:

- Be aware of the child's natural dignity and sense of self. *Do not initiate close contact. Do not initiate discussions of ethnic, religious, political or sexual matters.*
- Model appropriate behavior
- Gently remind students to stay on task and display courteous behavior
- Seek support from library staff in resolving behavioral issues

### Student Confidentiality:
You will learn student names and some personal information during the tutoring process. **You should treat this information as strictly confidential.**

Source: King County Library System

## Intellectual Freedom: How does it apply to you?

As a volunteer tutor in a public library, it is important that you provide all sides to a topic and allow the students to make their own conclusions.

It is critical that tutors do not attempt to persuade a student to agree with or accept a particular point of view, especially with regard to homework assignments related to politics, current events or historical topics.

## Note: Friends and Family at Study Zone

Friends, siblings and children of Study Zone tutors, who are in grades K-12, may attend Study Zone only if the tutor is able to provide equal attention to all of the other students at the table, as well.

**Tutors must maintain a professional approach when friends or family are present at the Study Zone table. Please do not socialize or chat during Study Zone sessions.**

If a tutor's friend or family member is not actively working on homework or is causing the tutors or other students to be distracted, then they will need to leave the Study Zone area.

## Note: Free Time Between Students

Occasionally, you may have free time between students. **Study Zone tutors are expected to stay until the end of their scheduled shift,** even if no students are present. Students can arrive near the end of a session looking for help.
- Feel free to read a book/magazine or do your own homework.
- **Please do not surf casually online.** The subtle change in body posture puts students off.

## Note: Headphones, "Google Glass" or similar devices

**Never wear headphones, earbuds or camera/video devices during a Study Zone session.** *Please remove these devices during your Study Zone session, even when students are not present.* These devices make the tutors appear less approachable and often make the students and/or parents uncomfortable.

This policy applies only to Study Zone tutors during their volunteer time in a Study Zone session (it is not applicable during personal time as a patron in the library).

*As patrons in the library, students attending Study Zone may choose to wear these devices and should not be asked to remove them.*

## Study Zone T-shirt & Badge:

KCLS provides each Study Zone volunteer a T-shirt and badge to be worn while volunteering. **Tutors must wear their Study Zone T-shirt every time they volunteer.**
- If you forget your T-shirt, please use the temporary T-shirt for that day, which can be found in the Study Zone Kit. Please keep your T-shirt clean and presentable.
- If your T-shirt is lost or is not presentable, or if you need a new size, please contact the program coordinator for a replacement.
- **PLEASE DO NOT GIVE YOUR T-SHIRT AWAY** to anyone who is not a current Study Zone tutor or donate Study Zone T-shirts to used clothing stores. Students trust the Study Zone T-shirt and we need to protect them from potential misuse. **Please destroy your T-shirt or return it to KCLS along with your badge to KCLS when you no longer need it.**

## Tutor Commitment:

The minimum commitment as a Study Zone volunteer is 2 hours, one day per week.
- Volunteer tutors are expected to continue their commitment through the end of the current academic semester.
- Contact the program coordinator if you are no longer able to tutor or need to change your assignment at any time.

## Tutor Attendance:

Consistent volunteer coverage is essential to the success of the Study Zone program. **Please make every effort to arrive on time and keep absences to an absolute minimum.**

Students depend on you to be there for the full two-hour session that has been advertised. **Study Zone tutors are expected to stay until the end of their scheduled shift,** even if no students are present. Students can arrive near the end of a session looking for help.

**Call the library directly if you will be late or absent for tutoring on a scheduled day.** Good communication with library staff is critical.

# Tutoring Guidelines:
## Behavior Management and Suggested Scripts

One of the reasons students act out is because they want your attention. Give each student your full attention during their time with you.

**You can ask a student to leave the Study Zone area if:**
- The student is no longer working productively on homework or skills building
- The student is disrupting the Study Zone area or is misbehaving in any way

**Volunteers are not expected to handle behavior problems directly.**

If you are comfortable asking a student to be quieter or to leave the area:
- Stay calm, don't take behavior personally
- Speak quietly and firmly
- Don't make threats, but identify options and consequences
  *"You have several choices, here they are…"*
- Take a time out rather than escalate
  *"Let's take a five minute break and then we can try again."*

Any continuation of a behavior issue should be addressed by a staff member. **Ask your Study Zone liaison or a staff member at the Information Desk to step in and address any behavioral issues that arise.**

## Students Not Doing Their Homework:

Don't feel bad if a student chooses not to do their homework. There are plenty of other students that do want your help. If a parent comes to collect their student from Study Zone and the homework was not done, that is an issue between the parent and student. As volunteer tutors in a public setting, we do not have the authority to "make" a student do their homework.

## When to Have Students Take a Break:

If a student is trying to understand their assignment but just seems to be getting more frustrated, take a break.

If a student is fidgeting, distracting other students, or otherwise unable to focus on their own work, have them take a break.

- Have the student take a break to walk around the library or get a drink of water.
- When they return, you can try to approach the assignment again.
- This will give the student a chance to relax and regroup, and may improve their ability to move forward in the assignment once their stress level has gone down.

Some students will pretend that they are confused or cannot find the answer.  This is generally for one of two purposes:
- To get a response from the tutor (annoyance, anger, frustration, impatience, or some other negative feeling)
- To avoid making an effort to learn by getting the tutor to provide the answer outright

Tell the student that you understand how difficult this assignment is.  Make it clear that you cannot give them the answer.  Have them take a break and come back to try again.

If a student asks you to complete a homework assignment for them, calmly and firmly offer to help them, but make it clear that you are not allowed to complete any homework for them.

## Sending Students Back to the Teacher:

If a homework question or assignment cannot be answered by a Study Zone tutor or KCLS librarian, **encourage the student to ask their teacher for clarification.** *This can be a frightening thing for students to do, and they will need some cheering on. Being able to communicate with a teacher is a very important, and an often avoided, skill.*

If you see the student often, **check back with them and ask how it went.**

You can fill out a Homework Referral for the student. *A note can give a student a boost of confidence when approaching their teacher.*

## How to Tell a Student They Need to Practice:

If you notice a student is struggling in specific skill areas, it is okay to encourage them to practice those skills.

Keep it positive and encouraging as much as possible. Students are usually more open to these suggestions when they do not feel they are being criticized.

Suggested script:

"Let's work on fractions today so we can get your homework done, but one thing that will really help is to practice your basic multiplication and division skills. It seems like you're struggling there and it will make other math harder down the road."

Then encourage them to practice those skills at home and to come back to Study Zone with worksheets from school or home to practice further.

## Special Needs and High Demand Students:

Study Zone is a group setting and students need to work independently and take turns working with the tutor.

Study Zone is not suitable for students who need a lot of intensive supervision and tutoring.

As a general rule, only Study Zone tutors and students should be at the Study Zone table.

However, if you feel the parent would be able help their student stay on task and would not be disruptive to the rest of the Study Zone session, you can choose to make an exception and invite the parent to stay at the table and help their child along.

If a student with special needs cannot focus on their work independently or with the help of a parent or continues to interrupt the Study Zone session, then they may be requiring more individual attention than we can realistically provide.

**Ask your Study Zone liaison or a staff member at the Information Desk to step in.** They can let the parent know that Study Zone is a group setting and is not really suitable for students who need a lot of intensive supervision and tutoring and that it seems like this student needs more help and direct attention than we are able to provide.

## Personal Boundaries:

Some students will come to a tutor for attention and social interaction. These students may seem "clingy" or demand attention from the tutor.

You can let the student know that they are welcome to study at the tables with you, but that they cannot interrupt while you assist other students.

Don't be afraid to be honest. Let a student know when they are being too pushy and be firm that they need to work on their own unless they have a question they really cannot answer themselves.

**Okay:**

- High fives
- Hand shakes
- Fist bumps
- Side hugs
- Gentle touch on the arm

**Not Okay:**

- "Bear" hugs
- Giving or receiving back rubs
- Giving or receiving kisses
- Allowing students to sit on your lap
- Spanking, hitting, grabbing or shaking someone in anger
- Depending on cultural background, patting the head may be inappropriate

## Student Illness:

Runny noses, every day cold symptoms and even mild tummy aches don't usually warrant turning a student away.

For everyday colds, runny noses, etc., bottles of hand sanitizer are available for the Study Zone Kit.

If a student has a fever, has thrown up or has diarrhea they should not be attending Study Zone.

If a student looks truly sick (not just a runny nose), you can suggest to the parent to keep him home. If a parent is not present, you can address the issue directly with the student.

If the symptoms are less obvious or the student just looks generally under the weather, you can ask the student if they are feeling okay first. Then if they say they don't feel good, suggest they go home.

**Suggested Script:** "We appreciate your student's dedication to Study Zone, but it looks like some rest at home might be in order."

# Tutoring Guidelines:
## English Language Learners

**If a student is new to the English language and they are having difficulty communicating:**

- Work patiently to convey your meaning.

- Speak slowly and clearly.
  *This allows the student time to translate more easily.*

- Choose basic English words.

- Speaking louder will generally not help.

- Try writing it down. *Many students read and write a second language better than they may be able to speak it.*

- Try different words that mean the same thing. One of them may be easier for that student to understand.

- Ask the student to explain the assignment to you in order to gauge that they understand.

- If you speak the student's first language, try first to provide assistance in English. *This will give the student an opportunity to practice their English skills.*

If a student needs a tutor who can speak their first language, **use the Tutor Languages list**, available online at **www.kcls.org/studyzone.**

Refer to the Tutoring Guidelines Files on your MyVolunteerPage.com account welcome screen for more detailed tips and examples.

# Tutoring Guidelines:
## Addressing Signs of Abuse

**If a child tells you that they are being abused or shares personal experiences that cause you to suspect that they may have been abused report the incident to the onsite managing librarian immediately.**

KCLS staff members are not required to report suspected or reported abuse, but the manager or supervisor in the library will further assess the situation and contact appropriate authorities if necessary.

**Don't:**
- Panic, act shocked or upset
- Blame or be judgmental
- Probe for details
- Make promises to help
- Say you won't tell anybody

**Do:**
- Stay calm and listen carefully
- Tell the child you believe him/her
- Tell the child that they did the right thing in telling you
- Tell the child that he/she is not to blame for what happened
- Tell the child that you are required to tell your supervisor

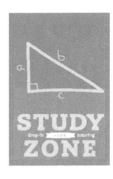

# Tutoring Guidelines:
## Essential Homework Skills

## Essential Homework Skills:

- **Follow the Assignment Instructions**: Make sure the student has read the instructions and is actually following them.

- **Understand the Question:** If a student does not grasp the original question or does not understand one or more key words in the question, they will not be able to answer it properly.

- **Complete Answers:** Make sure the student is actually answering the question that was asked. Are they simply plugging in loosely related information, but not fully addressing the original question?

- **Finding Information in a Book:** Show the student how to use the Index or Table of Contents. Only look for the answer in the area of the textbook or novel that would contain that information. What chapter did they read in class today?

- **Reading Comprehension:** Have the student review the questions before they begin reading any assigned text. Looking for information and taking notes as you read can increase comprehension and reduce the need to re-read the text again.

## Helping Students Better Understand the Subject They Are Studying:

Try not to rush the student

Do not take it personally when the student does not understand your explanations.

**Try to explain the subject in a different way.**
Each person learns differently and sometimes there are communication problems that get in the way.
- Repeat the information to the student again using different words and/or metaphors.
- Paraphrase what you are hearing from the student. *I heard you say you don't like reading aloud, can you tell me more about that?*
- Help the student express what they are feeling. *It sounds like you are really frustrated and anxious about this assignment.*

**Have the student try to explain what she or he thinks the answers is. Listen to their response.** You may be able to pick up a pattern that is leading them in the wrong direction.

**When a student asks for assistance, point them to the page or section of the textbook that contains the information they need.**
Locate the page first, then have the student find the exact information they are looking for.
If the student has difficulty identifying what they are looking for, point out the key elements of the question or assignment to provide clues to the information they are looking for.

# Staff Manual Excerpts

## Expectations of Volunteer Tutors

### Commitment
Homework Help volunteers are asked to make a minimum commitment of 2 hours for one day per week at the same location for one academic semester. All Homework Help volunteers should fill out timesheets each day they tutor at the library.

### Absences
Tutors are expected to establish a schedule each semester and keep to it. Please ask your site supervisor and lead tutor to discuss how you can let them know when a planned or unplanned (such as illness) absence occurs.

### Volunteer Badges
Please wear your volunteer ID badge. These badges serve to identify you as a member of the library's team to library patrons and staff.

### Academic and Community Service Credit for volunteer tutors
ServiceCorps, Service Learning students, and high school juniors and seniors are eligible to use Homework Help volunteer hours to earn community service or service learning credit toward academic classes. Records of your service will be kept for at least six years. Submit requests for verification of your volunteer hours to the Volunteer Office at 612-543-8579.

### Comply with Library Policies
*Data Privacy*
Information you learn about patrons while working at the library must be kept confidential. This is especially important to keep in mind when speaking with patrons about the information they came to the library to find. The Hennepin County Data Privacy Policy notes the value of intellectual freedom and patrons' right to open inquiry without having their subjects of interest examined or scrutinized by others.

*Patron Use of Library Spaces*
Patrons are expected to understand that library spaces are shared by many, to conduct themselves in a safe and orderly way and allow others to do the same. Any problems should be referred to library staff.

### Comply with the Hennepin County Volunteer Agreement
The volunteer agreement that you sign at the beginning of the term outlines the following expectations regarding your interaction with students in the library. These guidelines have been established for the protection of both volunteers and students.

I will provide assistance respectfully.
I understand that my relationship to the student is professional and not personal.
All contact between volunteers and students will take place in the library during Homework Help hours.
I will refrain from engaging with students over social media.
I will keep information about the students confidential.
Any problems will be referred to library staff for resolution.
I will be on time as scheduled, and notify the library if unable to work.
I will consult with library staff for specific rules regarding my library.

Source: Hennepin County Library

## Expectations of Homework Helpers

**Build Positive Relationships with Students:**

Offer encouragement and guidance for students. Be patient, compassionate, flexible, creative and willing to use a variety of methods to promote understanding of homework assignments and concepts.

Help motivate students by supporting self-confidence. Understand that effective praise is specific, rather than general, and attributes the student's success to his/her efforts and abilities.

Demonstrate a genuine appreciation and respect for students from diverse cultures. Learn about their cultures and values.

Use your active listening skills and ask open-ended questions to engage students in planning and completing their homework assignments. Allow enough time for students to think through questions instead of continually asking questions.

Set high expectations for students. Research shows that teacher and tutor expectations are a great predictor of a student's success.

Remain optimistic and supportive, even when a student is discouraged.

Let go of your assumptions and avoid patronizing behavior. Be supportive and treat each student as a unique individual.

Rely on your sense of humor. Tutoring should be a fun and engaging experience for students and volunteers!

**Maintain Boundaries with Students:**

- Share personal information only when it is relevant to the homework assignment or college/career mentoring that you are offering for students.
- You may not give your home address, phone number or email address to students. Please do not communicate with students on Facebook, Instagram, Twitter or other social media.
- You may not transport students in your car or socialize with students outside of the Library.
- If a student requests your help with resolving a personal, financial or health issue, refer the student to your Homework Help liaison or the branch's assistant manager for assistance with locating appropriate community resources.
- You may not accept gifts or money from students or their family members.
- You are encouraged to be friendly with students at the Library, but always keep in mind that your relationship with students is a professional one.
- When you are not sure about what is appropriate, please speak with your Homework Help liaison or the Volunteer Services Coordinator for guidance.

**Respect Students' Privacy:**

- You may be aware of confidential personal information about students. **You may not share personal information about a student with other volunteers and individuals outside of the Library.** If you have a concern about a student, please speak with your Homework Help liaison or the branch's assistant manager.

**Communicate with the Library's Staff and Volunteers:**

- Keep in regular contact with your Homework Help liaison. Email is the best way to communicate with your liaison when you have questions, suggestions or a schedule change.

- The Seattle Public Library provides an email distribution list for you to communicate with other Homework Helpers and the staff liaison at your branch. You can share questions, suggestions of tutoring tips and resources, requests for supplies and inform others of your schedule changes. **When you must cancel a scheduled Homework Help session, you can either request a substitute or exchange shifts with another volunteer.** Please use the email distribution list for communication only related to Homework Help. (Please keep in mind that all email that is sent through City of Seattle servers is subject to public disclosure.)

- If you must cancel a scheduled Homework Help session because of illness or an emergency, please call the branch to inform the staff and then request a substitute Homework Helper by sending an email to your branch's email distribution list.

- Check in with Library staff when you arrive and when you leave. After checking in, please write your volunteer start time on your volunteer time-sheet and pick up a volunteer badge. Please sign out and return the badge when you leave. If you forget to add your Homework Help volunteer hours to your time-sheet, you can email your hours to the Volunteer Services Coordinator at the end of the month.

- The Library will provide supplies (e.g. rulers, graph paper, calculators) for you to use at Homework Help. Contact your Homework Help liaison when supplies need to be replenished.

- The Library will also provide training opportunities for Homework Helpers throughout the school year. If you would like to suggest training topics, please contact Josie Watanabe at Josie.Watanabe@spl.org.

## Homework Help Basics

"I've learned that people will forget what you said, people will forget what you did, but people will never forget how you made them feel."

*Maya Angelou*

### Getting Started:

- Get to know students by asking them about their day, what they like and don't like, etc. Ask about their favorite classes and interests at school and what they enjoy learning about.

- Address each student by his or her first name. A good tip is to write the student's name down as soon as they tell you or use the sign-in sheet as a reference.

- Place yourself strategically between students. It's fine to ask students to move any time during the Homework Help session.

- Ask the student which homework assignment he/she would like to do first.

- Ask the student to explain his/her homework assignment to you and ask if you can take a look at the written assignment. This will give you the full picture on how to do the assignment and a good estimate on how much time it will take for the student to complete the work.

- Engage the student in thinking about the homework assignment by asking open-ended questions and listening carefully. Read the materials provided by teachers.

- If several students request homework assistance at the same time, plan what order would be best for all. Inform each student of when you will be able to provide assistance. You can help a student get started on an assignment and return after assisting other students.

- Keep in mind that there are different types of learners: auditory, visual, etc. Use a variety of methods to promote understanding of homework assignments and concepts.

- If the student does not understand a concept, he/she may have made an assumption that is leading him/her astray. Ask open-ended questions to identify misconceptions.

- Relate problems (especially math) to the real world. Use clear and concrete examples.

- Be patient and allow the student enough time to think about answers.

- Ask the student to explain the problem to you. Often understanding comes through the process of explaining.

- Don't overwhelm the student by giving too much information.

- If the student needs assistance with using the Library Catalog, databases or finding reference materials, please refer him/her to a librarian.

- If the student did not bring the textbook or materials needed to complete the assignment, ask if other students are working on the same assignment. You can also ask the librarians if they have resources that can help the student.

# Letter of Intent

**SAMPLE LETTER OF INTENT**

*[Date]*

Dear *(Company Name Here),*

The _____ Library offers a wide variety of services to the citizens of *(your city or county name here).* To ensure the library is providing the best services for the community, we are constantly updating our collections and programs. With this in mind, we are currently developing a homework center for those students in grades 6-12.

Providing homework centers for middle school and high school students will allow the education process to be continued and developed outside of the classroom. The _____ Library has enlisted the help of the local school district to review and purchase resources to start a homework center in our _____ Branch Library. Currently, the neighborhood where this library is located, has *(number)* students in the 6-12 grade range that would be able to use this fantastic resource. While the homework center would be free to all participants, we need additional financial support beyond the amount the library's program and services budget can provide. These additional funds will enable us to offer an outstanding, high quality homework center.

With the help of *(business name here)*, the library can provide a space that would be informative and productive to our citizens in middle and high school. The _____ Library hopes to receive $10,000 in donations to help fund our homework center. This donated amount will be used to purchase materials to be used for homework, such as dictionaries, provide materials for students to complete their homework, such as protractors and calculators, and cover the cost of printing and advertising. Your generosity and support for this program will be acknowledged in the library's printed literature, which will include flyers and advertisements in the local newspaper.

The _____ Library is committed to fostering a life-long love of books, reading, and education for the residents of the City of _____. Your sponsorship truly supports this goal, and we hope that you will see this request as a unique opportunity to support literacy and lifelong learning in our community.

Thank you for your time and consideration.

Jane Doe
Director of Libraries
_____ Library

Source: Sian Brannon and WyLaina Hildreth. 2011. Teen Homework Centers—Minimum Resources for Most Budgets. Texas Library Journal 87 (Spring): 19–25.

16 Teen Homework Centers – Minimum Resources for Most Budgets

# STUDY ZONE
### drop-in FREE tutoring

# HOMEWORK REFERRAL
## ADDITIONAL SUPPORT NEEDED

**Dear Teacher:**

Your student attended Study Zone to work with our tutors on the homework assignment indicated below.

We had difficulty assisting with this assignment because necessary information was missing. We encourage students to return to their teachers and begin a dialogue that will help them to better understand their homework. Please clarify the assignment for this student and we would be happy to help them complete it.

**Student Name:**_____

**Tutor:**_____ **Library:**_____

**Today's Date:**_____

**Homework Assignment:**_____

**Tutor's Notes:**_____

_____

_____

_____

Source: King County Library System

Dear Teachers and School Staff,

Monterey County Free Libraries (MCFL) welcomes you and your students back to school! The Marina Branch Library is here to help you and your students have a successful school year. We have many resources available for students and teachers.

We know how important homework is for student achievement. Our Homework Center is open to assist students with homework after school. Homework Centers are FREE and have staff to help students on a drop-in basis. MCFL also provides access to online homework help "Help Now" to assist students on a vast array of subjects. The service is available every day from 1pm-11pm and is accessible from home with a library card and an internet connection. Please contact the library at 831-883-7507 for more information about these services.

Please help us spread the word about these services to your students. We invite you to circulate the included flyers throughout your library and classrooms. Together we can make this the most successful school year yet!

Marina Branch Library Homework Center hours;

| Tuesday | 2:30-8:00pm |
| Wednesday | 1:30-7:00pm |
| Thursday | 1:00-5:00pm |

Sincerely,

Marina Library Staff
190 Seaside Circle
Marina, CA 93933
831-883-7507

Source: Monterey County Free Libraries

# Registration Forms

## Homework Help Guidelines

Dear Parents and Students:

We are so glad you've requested homework help time with a tutor at the Los Alamos branch of the Santa Maria Public Library. All of our tutors are working with students for free, so we need to respect our volunteers' time by following these guidelines:

1. It is the parents' responsibility to make sure their child is at the library on time to meet their tutor. We have scheduled the meetings based on the times you have requested; if there's a problem, contact the tutor to reschedule.

2. If your child cannot attend the tutoring session, you must contact the tutor ahead of time so that our volunteers do not come to the library for no reason.

3. We have many students on our waiting list, so if your child misses two sessions without notifying the tutor, another student will be assigned to the tutor. We want to help as many students as we can.

4. Make sure your child brings his/her homework to each session. If your child does not want to attend the tutoring sessions, please let the tutor or Vickie Gill know right away.

We truly appreciate that so many residents of Los Alamos have volunteered their time to guide students through their homework assignments. This is a wonderful program for kids who are motivated to improve their reading, writing and math skills. Please feel free to contact me or Brenda Galvez if you have any questions.

Sincerely,


Vickie Gill, Homework Help Coordinator
805-287-6981

I have read and understand the guidelines for participating in the Los Alamos Homework Help program.

Parent Signature: _____

Date: _____

Student's Name:_____

Source: Santa Maria Public Library, Los Alamos branch

## Homework Help Guidelines

Estimados Padres y Estudiantes:

Estamos tan contentos de que ha solicitado el tiempo de tarea ayuda con un tutor en la Biblioteca Pública de Los Alamos. Todos nuestros tutores están trabajando con los estudiantes de forma gratuita, por lo que tenemos que respetar el tiempo de nuestros voluntarios siguiendo estas pautas:

1. Es responsabilidad de los padres para asegurarse de que su hijo se encuentra en la biblioteca de tiempo para cumplir con su tutor. Hemos programado las reuniones en base a los tiempos que ha requerido; Si hay un problema, póngase en contacto con el tutor para reprogramar.

2. Si su hijo no puede asistir a la sesión de tutoría, debe ponerse en contacto con el tutor antes de tiempo para que nuestros voluntarios no vengan a la biblioteca sin ninguna razón.

3. Tenemos muchos estudiantes en lista de espera, por lo que si su hijo no recibe dos sesiones sin notificar al tutor, otro estudiante se le asignará al tutor. Queremos ayudar a tantos estudiantes como podamos.

4. Asegúrese de que su hijo lleva a su / sus deberes de cada sesión. Si su hijo no quiere asistir a las sesiones de tutoría, por favor, deje que el tutor o Vickie Gill saber enseguida.

Nosotros realmente apreciamos que tantos residentes de Los Alamos han ofrecido su tiempo para guiar a los estudiantes a través de sus tareas. Este es un programa maravilloso para los niños que están motivados para mejorar sus habilidades de lectura, escritura y matemáticas. Por favor, siéntase libre de ponerse en contacto conmigo o Brenda Gálvez si tiene alguna pregunta.

Sinceramente,

Vickie Gill, Homework Help Coordinador
805-287-6981

He leído y entendido las instrucciones para participar en el programa de ayuda con la tarea de Los Álamos.

Firma de los padres: _____

Fecha: _____

Nombre del estudiante _____

## Mission Viejo Library
### Homework Help
### 2016-2017 Registration Form
### Program Information

The Homework Help program provides homework assistance to students in Grades 2 through 6 with trained Library volunteers. Volunteers are homework helpers who assist students in understanding and completing their assignments, as well as teaching about various resources available at the Library. Helpers do not guarantee completion of the homework assignments. Homework Help is a free resource. Volunteers will not use Mission Viejo Library Homework Help to advertise any personal tutoring business. Homework Help is open during the academic year on Wednesdays from 3:30 through 5:30 p.m. It will not be available during school vacations.

<u>PLEASE BE ON TIME.</u> Your slot will be released to the next waiting student if you don't arrive at the appointed time.
(Please print.)
Student Last Name:_____ First Name:_____

Age:_____Grade:_____ Library Card #:_____

Parent or Guardian Name:_____

Home Phone #:_____ Cell #:_____

Teacher's Name:_____ School Attended:_____

<u>PARENT COMMITMENT:</u>
My child and I know that Library rules must be followed. The Homework Help program is not a child care program and I (or my child's caregiver, sibling, etc.) agree to stay in the Library building for the duration of my child's Homework Help session. Children who are disruptive will be removed from the Study Room and their parent will be notified. _____ (please initial)

I understand that in order to serve as many students as possible, I must call to cancel if my child won't be able to attend a scheduled appointment, for whatever reason (illness, vacation, no homework, etc.) If I do not call to cancel and this happens three times, my child will need to wait for 12 weeks before scheduling to attend Homework Help sessions again. _____ (please initial)

I give permission for my child to participate in the Homework Help program.

Date:_____ Parent Signature:_____

Student Signature:_____

Source: Mission Viejo Library

Mission Viejo Library
100 Civic Center
Mission Viejo, CA 92691

Dear Parent:

Your child has signed up to participate in the Mission Viejo Library's free Tutoring Program. We would like to provide you with the following information about this program.

- The Tutoring Program is free and takes place in the Bill Price Conference Room.
- Tutors are Mission Viejo Library Volunteers.
- Participation in a tutoring session is by appointment. Appointments are made at the Adult Reference Desk, or by calling 830-7100, extension 5105.
- No personal information (telephone numbers, etc.) is given to either tutors or students.
- The Mission Viejo Library is not responsible for your child's attendance or participation in the Tutoring Program.
- Volunteer tutors will not use the Mission Viejo Library's Tutoring Program to advertise any personal tutoring business.
- Tutoring sessions are one hour in length and tutors do not correct homework or give answers to tests.
- Due to the popularity of the Tutoring Program, there is no guarantee that your child will always be able to meet with a tutor.
- Students who participate in the Mission Viejo Library's Tutoring Program must have a Mission Viejo Library card. Library cards are free.

I _____ give permission for my child, _____, to participate in the Mission Viejo Library's Tutoring Program and agree to abide by the program's policies.

Date: _____ MVL card_____

Please have your child return this completed form to the Mission Viejo Library Reference Desk.
Thank you.

# Survey Instruments

1

## CHICAGO PUBLIC LIBRARY

**Library Branch:** _____       **Age:** _____

### TEACHER IN THE LIBRARY SURVEY: CHILD

1. Please select one or more reasons why you take part in the Teacher in the Library program:

   ○ To do homework
   ○ My parents make me
   ○ To get help with reading
   ○ To get help with math
   ○ To get help for a test
   ○ Because my friend is going

   ○ Because I have nothing else to do
   ○ To get better grades
   ○ There's no one else to help me with homework after school
   ○ Other _____

2. I feel safe when I come to Teacher in the Library.

   Agree          Disagree          Don't Know

3. I think the Teacher in the Library wants me to succeed.

   Agree          Disagree          Don't Know

4. Since coming to Teacher in the Library, I complete my homework assignments.

Source: Chicago Public Library

2

Agree      Disagree      Don't Know

5. My homework assignment are less frustrating since coming to Teacher in the Library.

Agree      Disagree      Don't Know

6. I feel more comfortable talking to adults (teachers, librarians, parents, etc.) since coming to Teacher in the Library.

Agree      Disagree      Don't Know

7. I feel better about doing homework since coming to Teacher in the Library.

Agree      Disagree      Don't Know

8. My afterschool work habits have improved since coming to Teacher in the Library.

Agree      Disagree      Don't Know

9. I feel more confident about myself as a learner since coming to Teacher in the Library.

Agree      Disagree      Don't Know

10. I feel better about going to school since coming to Teacher in the Library.

Agree      Disagree      Don't Know

# CHICAGO PUBLIC LIBRARY

**Library Branch:** _____        **Child's Age:** _____

## TEACHER IN THE LIBRARY SURVEY:
## PARENT/GUARDIAN

1. Please select one or more reasons why your child uses Teacher in the Library:

   ○ To do homework
   ○ Because I make him/her come
   ○ To get help with reading
   ○ To get help with math
   ○ To get help for a test
   ○ Because his/her friend is going
   ○ Because he/she has nothing else to do
   ○ To get better grades
   ○ There's no one else to help with homework after school
   ○ Other _____

2. When using Teacher in the Library services, your child feels safe and supported.

   Agree            Disagree            Don't Know

3. Since using Teacher in the Library Services, your child completes his/her homework.

   Agree            Disagree            Don't Know

4. Since using Teacher in the Library Services, your child feels less frustrated about his/her homework assignments.

   Agree            Disagree            Don't Know

5. Since using Teacher in the Library Services, your child feels more comfortable communicating with adults (teachers, parents, caregivers, librarians, etc.).

2

Agree             Disagree          Don't Know

6. Since using Teacher in the Library Services, your child has an improved attitude towards homework.

   Agree             Disagree          Don't Know

7. Since using Teacher in the Library Services, your child's afterschool work habits have improved.

   Agree             Disagree          Don't Know

8. Since using Teacher in the Library Services, your child shows more confidence in himself/herself as a learner.

   Agree             Disagree          Don't Know

9. Since using Teacher in the Library Services, your child shows a better attitude towards school.

   Agree             Disagree          Don't Know

10. As a parent, have you ever received guidance, resources or support from the Teacher in the Library program to help you as you work with your child with his/her homework?

    Yes                    No

11. How often does your child participate in Teacher in the Library

    - ○
    - ○ Daily
    - ○ 2-3 times per week
    - ○ 1 time per week
    - ○ 1-2 times per month
    - ○ This is my child's first time

**Please share any additional comments:**

DATE: _____
ID: _____
Total Student Visits _____

### PARENT/GUARDIAN HOMEWORK CENTER SURVEY
### EXIT

1. Please tell us the reasons why your child comes to the Homework Center by indicating which of the following apply:

- To do homework

- Because I make him/her come

- To get help with reading

- To get help with math

- To get help for a test

- Because his/her friend is going

- Because he/she has nothing else to do

- To get better grades

- There's no one else to help with homework after school

- Other _____

2. Please tell us the things you like the best about your child coming to the Homework Center by indicating which of the following apply:

- Getting help with homework

- Getting help with reading

- Getting help with math

- Reading with a tutor/coach

- Working with a tutor

- Playing educational games

- Doing homework with other kids

3. Since coming to the homework center, has the center helped them understand their homework better?

Strongly Disagree    Disagree    Agree    Strongly Agree    N/A

4. Since coming to the homework center, have your child's grades improved?

Strongly Disagree    Disagree    Agree    Strongly Agree    N/A

5. Since coming to the homework center, does your child have a better attitude about school?

Strongly Disagree    Disagree    Agree    Strongly Agree    N/A

6. Since coming to the homework center, are your evenings at home less stressful concerning Homework?

Strongly Disagree    Disagree    Agree    Strongly Agree    N/A

7. Since coming to the homework center, does your child regularly spend time every day on Homework?

Strongly Disagree    Disagree    Agree    Strongly Agree    N/A

8. My child feels comfortable going to library staff for help.

Strongly Disagree    Disagree    Agree    Strongly Agree    N/A

9. My child feels welcome here.

Strongly Disagree    Disagree    Agree    Strongly Agree    N/A

10. Participating in the homework center has helped my child learn to interact well with other children.

Strongly Disagree    Disagree    Agree    Strongly Agree    N/A

11. Would you recommend the Homework Center to another parent or child?

Yes        No

12. What else do you feel is needed to make our Homework Center more useful?

13. Do you have any other questions/concerns about our Homework Center?

Thank you for your help in completing this survey.

Source: Cuyahoga County Public Library

# MCFL Homework Center User Survey 2014-2015

First Name _____ School _____ Grade _____ Date _____

**How often do you use the Homework Center? (circle one)**

Most/All days it is open    About once a week    A couple of times a month    Once a month or less

**When you get help at the Homework Center, who helps you? (circle all who help)**

HWC Coordinator    Library Staff    HWC Volunteers    Other Students    Parents/Family

**If you get help at the Homework Center, do you get the help you need? (Circle best answer)**

Almost always    Most of the time    Some of the time    Almost never

**Do you go anywhere else for homework help? (circle)**    Yes    No    **If Yes, Where?** _____

**Do you get homework help from anyone in your family?**    Often    Sometimes    No

**Here is a list of things people do at the Homework Center. Which of these things do you do?**
**(Mark boxes with an X )**

| ACTIVITY | I do this a lot | I do this sometimes | I don't do this |
|---|---|---|---|
| Get help with homework | ☐ | ☐ | ☐ |
| Help other students with their homework | ☐ | ☐ | ☐ |
| Look things up/do research for school reports or projects | ☐ | ☐ | ☐ |
| Get help with school reports or projects | ☐ | ☐ | ☐ |
| Work with other students on school projects | ☐ | ☐ | ☐ |
| Use computers | ☐ | ☐ | ☐ |
| Visit with friends/hang out | ☐ | ☐ | ☐ |

**Do you usually finish your homework when you do it at the library Homework Center?**

Always    Most of the time    Some of the time    Almost never

**Do you think coming to the Homework Center at the library has helped you in school?**    Yes    No    **If Yes, how?**

**Here is a list of things people do at the library. Which of these things do you know how to do?**
**(Mark boxes with an X )**

| ACTIVITY | I can do this on my own | I can do this with help | I don't know how |
|---|---|---|---|
| Look up information for school reports in books | ☐ | ☐ | ☐ |
| Look up information for school reports on the internet | ☐ | ☐ | ☐ |
| Use the library catalogue | ☐ | ☐ | ☐ |
| Find books on the shelves | ☐ | ☐ | ☐ |
| Know how to check out a book | ☐ | ☐ | ☐ |
| Know whom to ask for help | ☐ | ☐ | ☐ |
| Know how to get books that are not in **this** library | ☐ | ☐ | ☐ |

**Do you use the library when you don't have homework?**    Yes    No

Source: Monterey County Free Libraries

# Encuesta para Usuarios de los Centros de Tarea de MCFL 2014-2015

Primer Nombre _____ Escuela _____ Grado _____ Fecha _____

**¿Con qué frecuencia usas el Centro de Tarea? (circula uno)**

Todos los días que está abierto    Una vez por semana    Dos veces por mes    Una vez o menos por mes

**¿Cuando recibes ayuda en el Centro de Tarea, quién te ayuda? (circula todos los que te ayudan)**

Coordinador/a de Tarea    Personal de Biblioteca    Voluntarios    Otros Estudiantes    Padres/Familia

**¿Si recibes ayuda en el Centro de Tarea, recibes la ayuda que necesitas? (Circula la major respuesta)**

Casi siempre    La mayoría del tiempo    A veces    Casi nunca

**¿Vas a otro sitio para recibir ayuda con la tarea? (circula)**    Sí    No    **¿A donde?** _____

**¿Recibes ayuda para tu tarea de algún miembro de la familia?** Con frecuencia    A veces    No

**Aquí está una lista de cosas que puedes hacer en el Centro de Tarea. ¿Cuales de estas haces tú?**
(Marca las cajas con una X )

| ACTIVIDAD | Hago esto mucho | Hago esto a veces | No hago esto nunca |
|---|---|---|---|
| Buscar ayuda para la tarea | ☐ | ☐ | ☐ |
| Ayudar a otros estudiantes con sus tareas | ☐ | ☐ | ☐ |
| Buscar información para reportes y proyectos de la escuela | ☐ | ☐ | ☐ |
| Buscar ayuda con reportes y proyectos de la escuela | ☐ | ☐ | ☐ |
| Trabajar con otros estudiantes en proyectos de la escuela | ☐ | ☐ | ☐ |
| Usar las computadoras | ☐ | ☐ | ☐ |
| Hablar con amigos/pasar el rato | ☐ | ☐ | ☐ |

**¿Terminas tu tarea cuando la haces en el Centro de Tarea de la biblioteca?**

Siempre    La mayoría del tiempo    A veces    Casi nunca

**¿Crees tú que venir al Centro de Tareas en la biblioteca te está ayudando en la escuela?** Sí  No

**¿Si tu respuesta es Sí, como te está ayudando?**_____

**¿Aquí está una lista de cosas que se hacen en la Biblioteca. ¿Cuales de estas sabes hacer tú?**
(Marca las cajas con una X )

| ACTIVIDAD | Puedo hacer esto por mi cuenta | Puedo hacer esto con ayuda | No sé como hacer esto |
|---|---|---|---|
| Buscar información en los libros para reportes de la escuela | ☐ | ☐ | ☐ |
| Buscar información en el internet para reportes de la escuela | ☐ | ☐ | ☐ |
| Usar el catálogo de la Biblioteca | ☐ | ☐ | ☐ |
| Encontrar libros en los estantes | ☐ | ☐ | ☐ |
| Saber como sacar libros prestados | ☐ | ☐ | ☐ |
| Saber a quién pedirle ayuda | ☐ | ☐ | ☐ |
| Saber como pedir libros que no estan en esta biblioteca | ☐ | ☐ | ☐ |

**¿Usas la biblioteca cuando no tienes tarea?**    Sí    No

# MCFL Homework Center Parent Survey 2015-2016

Date: _____

Parents,

Monterey County Free Libraries is evaluating our Homework Center program. We would like your help in gathering some data. Please take a few minutes and answer the following questions. Your feedback is very important to us. Please fill out a separate survey for each child. Thank you.

**What grade is your child in?** _____ **First name of child?** _____

**1. There are many reasons that parents and children use the Homework Center. Please check all that apply to your child:**

_____ A. My child receives help with homework there
_____ B. My child finishes homework in the Homework Center
_____ C. My child is learning to use the library through coming to the Homework Center
_____ D. My child reads at the Homework Center
_____ E. My child is comfortable with the library staff and it is a safe place to hang out
_____ F. Other Reasons (Please List) _____

**2. Which of the above reasons for using the Homework Center would you rank the most important for your child?** Write in the letter from above _____

**3. Do you have a library card? (Circle)**   Yes     No

**4. Does your child have a library card?**  Yes     No

**5. Has using the Homework Center helped your child in school?**

Very Much     Somewhat     I Don't Know     No

**6. Has using the Homework Center helped your child develop study skills?**

Very Much     Somewhat     I Don't Know     No

**7. Has using the Homework Center helped your child develop confidence in doing homework?**

Very Much     Somewhat     I Don't Know     No

**8. Does your child use the library aside from the Homework Center?**     Yes     No

**9. Does your child check out materials (books, magazines, DVDs) from the library?**  Yes     No

**10. Please let us know your thoughts about the Homework centers?** _____

_____

**Can we use your name and comment for grantors?**     Yes     No

**Your Name (optional)** _____

*MCFL Updated 10/7/15*

**Encuesta para Padres de Usuarios de los Centros de Tarea de MCFL 2014-2015**

Fecha _____

Padres,

Las Bibliotecas Gratis del Condado de Monterey están evaluando el programa de los Centros de Tarea. Necesitamos su ayuda para recaudar algunos datos. Favor de tomar unos minutos para contestar las siguientes preguntas. Su opinión es muy importante para nosotros. Favor de llenar una encuesta separada para cada hijo/a. Gracias.

¿En qué grado está su hijo/a? _____     ¿Primer nombre de su hijo/a?_____

1. Hay muchas razones por las cuales los padres e hijos usan el Centro de Tarea. Favor de seleccionar todos los que aplican para su hijo/a:

_____ A. Mi hijo/a recibe ayuda con su tarea
_____ B. Mi hijo/a termina su tarea en el Centro de Tarea
_____ C. Mi hijo/a está aprendiendo a usar la biblioteca tan solo con venir al Centro de Tarea
_____ D. Mi hijo/a lee en el Centro de Tarea
_____ E. Mi hijo/a se siente cómodo con el personal de la biblioteca y es un lugar seguro para visitar
_____ F. Otras Razones (Por favor indique)
_____

2. ¿Cuál de las razones de arriba cree usted que es la más importante para su hijo/a al utilizar el Centro de Tarea? Escriba la letra _____

3. ¿Tiene usted una tarjeta de la biblioteca          □ Sí  □ No

4. ¿Tiene su hijo/a una tarjeta de la biblioteca?          □ Sí  □ No

5. ¿Le ha ayudado a su hijo/a en la escuela el utilizar el Centro de Tarea?

□ Mucho     □ Algo     □ No     □ No sé

6. ¿Le ha ayudado a su hijo/a en el desarrollo de habilidades de estudio el utilizar el Centro de Tarea?

□ Mucho     □ Algo     □ No     □ No sé

7. ¿Le ha ayudado a su hijo/a a desarrollar confianza en hacer su tarea el utilizar el Centro de Tarea?

□ Mucho     □ Algo     □ No     □ No sé

8. ¿Usa su hijo/a la biblioteca aparte del Centro de Tarea?          □ Sí     □ No

9. ¿Su hijo/a saca materiales prestados (libros, revistas, DVDs) de la biblioteca?  □ Sí  □ No

10. ¿Hay algo que usted cree que debería cambiar en el Centro de Tarea para hacerlo mejor para su hijo/a?_____

Date: _____                                                    Branch: _____

### *Do Your Homework @ the Library* Program: Survey for Grades K-5

Please help us by completing this survey. (Circle) your answers. Thank you!

| | Strongly Agree | Agree | Neutral | Disagree | Strongly Disagree | Don't Know |
|---|---|---|---|---|---|---|
| I like the Homework Center and the people who work here. | | | | | | ? |
| The tutor(s) and volunteer(s) are helpful. | | | | | | ? |
| I learned a lot while I was here. | | | | | | ? |
| This is the best place outside of school to get help with my homework. | | | | | | ? |
| My grades have gone up because of the Homework Center. | | | | | | ? |
| I would tell other people about the Homework Center. | | | | | | ? |

**What grade are you in?** (Circle) your answer:     K      1st      2nd      3rd      4th      5th

**How did you first hear about the Homework Center?** (Circle) your answer.

   My School/Teacher      My Parent      Library      My friend      Internet      Other

**What do you like most about the Homework Center?**

_____

**What would make the Homework Center better?**     (Source: San Diego Public Library)

_____

Source: San Diego Public Library

Date: _____     Branch: _____

### *Do Your Homework @ the Library* Program: Survey for Grades 6 and up

If you have participated in the *Do Your Homework @ the Library* program, please take a few minutes to complete this brief survey. Circle your answers and return the survey to the library **by June 17, 2016.** Thank you!

| | Strongly Agree | Agree | Neutral | Disagree | Strongly Disagree | Don't Know ? |
|---|---|---|---|---|---|---|
| I like the Homework Center and the people who work here. | Strongly Agree | Agree | Neutral | Disagree | Strongly Disagree | Don't Know |
| The tutor(s) and volunteer(s) are helpful. | Strongly Agree | Agree | Neutral | Disagree | Strongly Disagree | Don't Know |
| I learned a lot while I was here. | Strongly Agree | Agree | Neutral | Disagree | Strongly Disagree | Don't Know |
| This is the best place outside of school to get help with my homework. | Strongly Agree | Agree | Neutral | Disagree | Strongly Disagree | Don't Know |
| My confidence in school has improved because of this program. | Strongly Agree | Agree | Neutral | Disagree | Strongly Disagree | Don't Know |
| My grades have improved because of this program. | Strongly Agree | Agree | Neutral | Disagree | Strongly Disagree | Don't Know |
| I would recommend this program to other students. | Strongly Agree | Agree | Neutral | Disagree | Strongly Disagree | Don't Know |
| I never used the library before I discovered this program. | Strongly Agree | Agree | Neutral | Disagree | Strongly Disagree | Don't Know |
| This program has made me aware of other library resources and services. | Strongly Agree | Agree | Neutral | Disagree | Strongly Disagree | Don't Know |

**\*\* Continued on other side\*\***

What grade are you in? (Circle your answer.)   6th   7th   8th   9th   10th   11th   12th

How did you first hear about the *Do Your Homework @ the Library* program? (Circle your answer.)

School/Teacher        Parent        Library        Friend        Internet        Other: _____

What do you like most about the *Do Your Homework @ the Library* program?

_____

What could the library do to improve the *Do Your Homework @ the Library* program?

_____

If the *Do Your Homework @ the Library* program has helped you in some way, please share your success story:

_____
_____
_____
_____
_____
_____

Would you be willing to talk further about this program? If so, please provide us with your name, email, and/or phone number in the space below:

_____

**Thank You!** ☺

Source: San Diego Public Library

Date: _____    Branch: _____

## *Do Your Homework @ the Library* Program: Parent Survey

If your child(ren) has/have participated in the *Do Your Homework @ the Library* program, please take a few minutes to complete this brief survey. Circle your answers and return the survey form to the library **by June 17, 2016**. Thank you!

| | Strongly Agree | Agree | Neutral | Disagree | Strongly Disagree | Don't Know |
|---|---|---|---|---|---|---|
| The Homework Center provides a safe environment for my child(ren). | Strongly Agree | Agree | Neutral | Disagree | Strongly Disagree | Don't Know |
| The tutor(s) and volunteer(s) are effective in providing homework help for my child(ren). | Strongly Agree | Agree | Neutral | Disagree | Strongly Disagree | Don't Know |
| There are an adequate number of tutor(s) and volunteer(s) available to help my child(ren). | Strongly Agree | Agree | Neutral | Disagree | Strongly Disagree | Don't Know |
| This program is the only place where my child(ren) can receive academic help outside of school. | Strongly Agree | Agree | Neutral | Disagree | Strongly Disagree | Don't Know |
| I feel my child(ren)'s overall confidence in academics has improved. | Strongly Agree | Agree | Neutral | Disagree | Strongly Disagree | Don't Know |
| My child(ren)'s grades have improved because of this program. | Strongly Agree | Agree | Neutral | Disagree | Strongly Disagree | Don't Know |
| This program has helped me feel more confident in assisting my child(ren) to learn. | Strongly Agree | Agree | Neutral | Disagree | Strongly Disagree | Don't Know |
| I am satisfied with this program. | Strongly Agree | Agree | Neutral | Disagree | Strongly Disagree | Don't Know |
| I would recommend this program to other parents/guardians. | Strongly Agree | Agree | Neutral | Disagree | Strongly Disagree | Don't Know |
| I never used the library before I discovered this program. | Strongly Agree | Agree | Neutral | Disagree | Strongly Disagree | Don't Know |
| This program has made me aware of other library resources and services. | Strongly Agree | Agree | Neutral | Disagree | Strongly Disagree | Don't Know |

**\*\* Continued on other side\*\***

What is/are the grade(s) of your child(ren)?  (Circle all that apply.)

K      1st      2nd      3rd      4th      5th      6th      7th      8th      9th      10th      11th      12th

How did you first hear about the *Do Your Homework @ the Library* program? (Circle your answer.)

School/Teacher        Child        Library        Friend        Internet        Other: _____

What do you like most about the *Do Your Homework @ the Library* program?

_____

What could the library do to improve the *Do Your Homework @ the Library* program?

_____

If the *Do Your Homework @ the Library* program has helped your child(ren), please share their success story:

_____

_____

_____

_____

_____

_____

_____

_____

Would you be willing to talk further about this program? If so, please provide us with your name, email, and/or phone number in the space below:

_____

**Thank you!** ☺

Source: San Diego Public Library

Fecha: _____     Sucursal Bibliotecaria: _____

## *Do Your Homework @ the Library* Program: Encuesta para los Padres de Familia

Si su(s) niño(s) han participado en el programa Do Your Homework at the Library, por favor tome unos minutos para llenar esta breve encuesta.  Póngale un (CIRCULO) a sus respuestas y regréselo a la biblioteca para el **17 de junio, 2016.**  ¡Gracias!

| | Fuerte Acuerdo | Acuerdo | Neutral | Desacuerdo | Fuerte Desacuerdo | No sé |
|---|---|---|---|---|---|---|
| El Centro de Tareas ofrece un ambiente seguro para mi(s) niños. | Fuerte Acuerdo | Acuerdo | Neutral | Desacuerdo | Fuerte Desacuerdo | No sé |
| Los tutores y voluntarios son efectivos dando ayuda con la tarea a mi(s) niños. | Fuerte Acuerdo | Acuerdo | Neutral | Desacuerdo | Fuerte Desacuerdo | No sé |
| Hay un número adecuado de tutores y voluntarios disponibles para darle ayuda a mi(s) niño(s). | Fuerte Acuerdo | Acuerdo | Neutral | Desacuerdo | Fuerte Desacuerdo | No sé |
| Este programa es el único lugar donde mi(s) niño(s) pueden recibir ayuda académica fuera de la escuela. | Fuerte Acuerdo | Acuerdo | Neutral | Desacuerdo | Fuerte Desacuerdo | No sé |
| Yo siento que la confianza total de mi(s) niño(s) en sus clases académicas ha mejorado. | Fuerte Acuerdo | Acuerdo | Neutral | Desacuerdo | Fuerte Desacuerdo | No sé |
| Mi(s) niño(s) han mejorado sus notas debido a este programa. | Fuerte Acuerdo | Acuerdo | Neutral | Desacuerdo | Fuerte Desacuerdo | No sé |
| Este programa me ha ayudado a sentirme con más confianza para asistir a mi(s) niño(s) en su aprendizaje. | Fuerte Acuerdo | Acuerdo | Neutral | Desacuerdo | Fuerte Desacuerdo | No sé |
| Yo estoy satisfecho/a con este programa. | Fuerte Acuerdo | Acuerdo | Neutral | Desacuerdo | Fuerte Desacuerdo | No sé |
| Yo recomendaría este programa a otros padres de familia o guardianes. | Fuerte Acuerdo | Acuerdo | Neutral | Desacuerdo | Fuerte Desacuerdo | No sé |
| Yo nunca había usado la biblioteca antes de haber descubierto este programa. | Fuerte Acuerdo | Acuerdo | Neutral | Desacuerdo | Fuerte Desacuerdo | No sé |
| Me he enterado de otros servicios y recursos de la biblioteca por este programa. | Fuerte Acuerdo | Acuerdo | Neutral | Desacuerdo | Fuerte Desacuerdo | No sé |

**\*\* Continua al otro lado\*\***

¿Cuál(es) es/son los grado(s) de su(s) niño(s)?  (Póngale un círculo a los grados).

K      1ro    2do    3ro    4to    5to    6to    7mo    8vo    9no    10mo    11vo    12vo

¿Cómo se dió cuenta acerca del programa *Do Your Homework @ the Library*? (Ponga un círculo a su respuesta.)

Escuela/Maestro      Niño      Biblioteca      Amigo      Internet      Otro: _____

¿Qué es lo que más le gusta acerca del programa *Do Your Homework @ the Library*?

_____

¿Qué podría hacer la biblioteca para mejorar el programa *Do Your Homework @ the Library*?

_____

Si el programa *Do Your Homework @ the Library* le ha ayudado a su(s) niño(s) en alguna manera, por favor comparta este suceso exitoso.

_____
_____
_____
_____
_____
_____
_____
_____

¿Le gustaría a Ud. hablar un poco más acerca de este programa?  Si es así, por favor denos su nombre, correo electrónico, y/o su número de teléfono en el espacio de abajo:

_____

**¡Gracias!** ☺

Source: San Diego Public Library

Ngày:_____                                    Thư Viện:_____

### *Do Your Homework @ the Library* Program: **Khảo Sát Phụ Huynh**

Nếu con em của quý vị đã tham gia vào chương trình *Do Your Homework @ the Library*, xin vui lòng dùng một chút thời gian để điền vào cái khảo sát ngắn này. Viết tròn câu đáp của quý vị và trả lại trang khảo sát này cho thư viện trước ngày **17 Tháng 5, 2016.**

| | Đồng Ý Hoàn Toàn | Đồng Ý | Trung Hòa | Không Đồng Ý | Hoàn Toàn Không Đồng Ý | Không Ý Kiến |
|---|---|---|---|---|---|---|
| Trung Tâm Làm Bài Tập cung cấp một môi trường an toàn cho con em. | Đồng Ý Hoàn Toàn | Đòng Ý | Trung Hòa | Không Đồng Ý | Hoàn Toàn Không Đồng Ý | Không Ý Kiến |
| Các thầy dạy kèm cung cấp sự giúp đỡ cho con em làm bài tập một cách hiệu quả. | Đồng Ý Hoàn Toàn | Đòng Ý | Trung Hòa | Không Đồng Ý | Hoàn Toàn Không Đồng Ý | Không Ý Kiến |
| Có đầy đủ thầy dạy kèm để giúp con em. | Đồng Ý Hoàn Toàn | Đòng Ý | Trung Hòa | Không Đồng Ý | Hoàn Toàn Không Đồng Ý | Không Ý Kiến |
| Chương trình này là nơi duy nhất ở ngoài trường các con em có thể nhận được sự giúp đỡ về học tập. | Đồng Ý Hoàn Toàn | Đòng Ý | Trung Hòa | Không Đồng Ý | Hoàn Toàn Không Đồng Ý | Không Ý Kiến |
| Tôi cảm thấy lòng tin về học tập của con em tôi có cải thiện. | Đồng Ý Hoàn Toàn | Đòng Ý | Trung Hòa | Không Đồng Ý | Hoàn Toàn Không Đồng Ý | Không Ý Kiến |
| Điểm học tập của con em tôi đã cải thiện bởi chương trình này. | Đồng Ý Hoàn Toàn | Đòng Ý | Trung Hòa | Không Đồng Ý | Hoàn Toàn Không Đồng Ý | Không Ý Kiến |
| Chương trình này đã giúp tôi có lòng tin để giúp đỡ con em tôi học tập. | Đồng Ý Hoàn Toàn | Đòng Ý | Trung Hòa | Không Đồng Ý | Hoàn Toàn Không Đồng Ý | Không Ý Kiến |
| Tôi thỏa mãn với chương trình này. | Đồng Ý Hoàn Toàn | Đòng Ý | Trung Hòa | Không Đồng Ý | Hoàn Toàn Không Đồng Ý | Không Ý Kiến |
| Tôi sẽ dới thiệu chương trình này với các phụ huynh khác. | Đồng Ý Hoàn Toàn | Đòng Ý | Trung Hòa | Không Đồng Ý | Hoàn Toàn Không Đồng Ý | Không Ý Kiến |
| Tôi chưa bao giờ dùng thư viện trước khi tìm thấy chương trình này. | Đồng Ý Hoàn Toàn | Đòng Ý | Trung Hòa | Không Đồng Ý | Hoàn Toàn Không Đồng Ý | Không Ý Kiến |
| Chương trình này cho tôi biết tới các tài nguyên và các dịch vụ khác của thư viện. | Đồng Ý Hoàn Toàn | Đòng Ý | Trung Hòa | Không Đồng Ý | Hoàn Toàn Không Đồng Ý | Không Ý Kiến |

**\*\* Tiếp Tục Ở Trang Sau \*\***

Con em quý vị ở lớp nào. (Viết tròn các lớp ứng dụng.)

K    1<sup>st</sup>    2<sup>nd</sup>    3<sup>rd</sup>    4<sup>th</sup>    5<sup>th</sup>    6<sup>th</sup>    7<sup>th</sup>    8<sup>th</sup>    9<sup>th</sup>    10<sup>th</sup>    11<sup>th</sup>    12<sup>th</sup>

Quý vị biết tới chương trình *Do Your Homework @ the Library* ở nơi đâu?  (Viết tròn các lớp ứng dụng.)

Nhà Trường/Thầy Dáo    Con em    Thư Viện    Bạn Bè    Trên Mạng    Nơi khác: _____

Khía cạnh nào quý vị thích trong chương trình *Do Your Homework @ the Library*?

_____

_____

_____

Thư Viện có thể làm gì để cải thiện chương trình *Do Your Homework @ the Library*?

_____

_____

_____

Nếu chương trình *Do Your Homework @ the Library* đã giúp được con em của quý vị, xin vui long chia sẻ câu chuyện thành công của quý vị:

_____

_____

_____

_____

_____

_____

_____

Nếu quý vị có muốn nói chuyện thêm vè chương trình này, xin cho email và/hoặc số điện thoại.

_____

_____

Source: San Diego Public Library

*Homework Help Student Survey 2016*

Your Library: _____  Your Grade: _____

Your School: _____

Why do you come to Homework Help? **Check 2 boxes.**

- ☐ I need help doing my homework.
- ☐ I need a place to go to do my homework.
- ☐ I don't understand the directions on my assignments.
- ☐ I like doing homework with my friends.
- ☐ I get great help from the tutors.
- ☐ Other: _____

2. What kind of homework do you need the most help with? **Check 2 boxes.**

- ☐ Math
- ☐ Reading
- ☐ Science
- ☐ Social Studies
- ☐ Writing
- ☐ College/Career Help
- ☐ Other: _____

3. What's the best thing about Homework Help? **Check 2 boxes.**
- ☐ I understand my homework.
- ☐ I get better grades.
- ☐ I wouldn't do any homework without the Homework Help program.
- ☐ I am more organized.
- ☐ I need homework supplies.
- ☐ I like the volunteers.
- ☐ Other: _____

4. How often do you come to Homework Help at the Library? **Check 1 box.**

- ☐ 4 times a week.
- ☐ 2-3 times a week.
- ☐ 1 time a week.
- ☐ Less than 1 time per week.

Source: Seattle Public Library

5. Do you attend an afterschool program other than Homework Help? **Check 1 box.**

☐ Yes
☐ No

6. Which language(s) are spoken at home?

☐ Amharic
☐ English
☐ Mandarin Chinese
☐ Oromo
☐ Somali
☐ Spanish
☐ Tigrinya
☐ Vietnamese
☐ Other: _____

7. Do you eat an afterschool HIP Homework Help snack at the library? **Check 1 box.**

☐ Often (3-4 times a week)
☐ Sometimes (1-2 times a week)
☐ Never (0 times a week)

8. If you only sometimes or never eat an afterschool HIP Homework Help snack, why is that? **Check 2 boxes.**

☐ I don't like the food that is served.
☐ I am not hungry (or I am waiting to eat dinner at home).
☐ The amount of food is just too small.
☐ I'd rather be in the library with friends.
☐ I feel uncomfortable or awkward getting a snack. Why? _____
☐ Other: _____

9. How can we make Homework Help better for you?

_____

Source: The Seattle Public Library

# BIBLIOGRAPHY

Adamec, Janet. 1990. "Homework Helpers: Making Study Time Quality Time." *Wilson Library Bulletin* 65 (September): 31–32.

Adams, Suellen S. 2010. "Marketing the Homework Center Digitally." *Young Adult Library Services* 8 (Winter 2010): 11–12.

American Library Association. 2016. "State of America's Libraries Report 2016." www.ala .org/news/state-americas-libraries-report-2016/issues-and-trends.

Aronson, Marc. 2014. "Text Sets: Your Chance to Lead the Common Core." *School Library Journal* (February 5). www.slj.com/2014/02/opinion/consider-the-source/ text-sets-your-chance-to-lead-the-common-core-consider-the-source/#_.

Aronson, Marc, and Susan M. Bartle. 2012. "Putting It All Together." *School Library Journal* 58 (November): 29–31.

Auerbach, Barbara. 1998. "Jenny and Her Trig Problem." *School Library Journal* 44 (January): 50.

Bailey, John F. 1999. "Qualifying Library Quality: A Homework Center Report Card." *American Libraries* 30 (September): 59–62.

Barack, Lauren. 2015. "MyLibraryNYC Brings Public Library Services to City Schools, 500,000+ Students." *School Library Journal* (June 24). www.slj.com/2015/06/ public-libraries/mylibrarynyc-brings-public-library-services-to-city-schools -500000-k-12-students/#_.

Brannon, Sian, and WyLaina Hildreth. 2011. "Teen Homework Centers—Minimum Re- sources for Most Budgets." *Texas Library Journal* 87 (Spring): 19–25.

Brewer, Rosellen. 1992. "Help Youth at Risk: A Case for Starting a Public Library Home- work Center." *Public Libraries* 31 (July/August): 208–12.

Brisson, Sarah-Ann. 2014. "Teens at the Brossard Public Library: A Necessary Adaptation of Space and Services." *Feliciter* 60 (December): 23–25.

Brown, Jane R. 2002. *Monterey County Free Libraries Homework Center Evaluation 2001–2002: Evaluation Manual.* Foundation for Monterey County Free Libraries. www.co .monterey.ca.us/library/images/hwc.pdf.

Callaci, Dorothy. 2015. "Special Delivery: MyLibraryNYC Opens Up Endless Possibilities for Cash-Strapped Schools." Unified Federation of Teachers (January 8). www.uft.org/news-stories/special-delivery.

Carnegie Council on Adolescent Development. 1992. *A Matter of Time: Risk and Opportunity in the Nonschool Hours.* New York: Carnegie Corporation.

"Case Study: Detroit Public Library." 2013. Tutor.com. www.tutor.com/cmspublicfiles/ WWW/DetroitCaseStudy.pdf.

Chamberlayne, Charles. 2014. "Mayor Aligns Broad Coalition to Support Expanded Library Hours & Afterschool Program in One San Diego Budget." (April 22). www .sandiego.gov/mayor/news/releases/20140422_LoganHeightsLibraryRelease.

City of Chicago, Mayor's Press Office. 2013. "Chicago Public Library Now Offers Largest Homework Help Program in Nation." (October 3). www.cityofchicago.org/city/en/ depts/mayor/press_room/press_releases/2013/october_2013/chicago_public _librarynowofferslargesthomeworkhelpprograminnatio.html.

City of Santa Clarita Public Library. 2015. "Annual Report, Fiscal Year 2014–2015." www.santaclaritalibrary.com/files/2013/08/SCPL-Annual-Report-2015.pdf.

Corburn, James. 2005. *Street Science: Community Knowledge and Environmental Health Justice.* Cambridge, MA: MIT Press.

De Rosa, Cathy, Joanne Cantrell, Matthew Carlson, Peggy Gallagher, Janet Hawk, and Charlotte Sturtz. 2010. "Perceptions of Libraries, 2010: Context and Community; A Report to the OCLC Membership." Dublin, OH: OCLC. www.oclc.org/en/ reports/2010perceptions.html.

Dunmore, Angela J., and Karen Cropsey Hardiman. 1987. "'My Turn' Boosts Teen Self-Esteem: Public Library/Public School Project Ties Students as Tutors." *American Libraries* 18 (October): 786, 788.

Edwards, Margaret A. 1969. *A Fair Garden and the Swarm of Beasts: The Library and the Young Adult.* Chicago: American Library Association.

Elam, Lynn, Tiffany Auxier, and Becca Boland. 2009. "How to Get Nearly 1,000 Teens into Your Library in Five Days or Less." *Voice of Youth Advocates* 32 (October): 288–89.

Favot, Sarah. 2016. "Broad Foundation Donates $1 Million to LA Public Libraries." *L.A. School Report* (August 30). laschoolreport.com/broad-foundation-donates -1-million-to la-public-libraries.

Garcia, June, and Sandra Nelson. 2007. *Public Library Service Responses.* Chicago: Public Library Association.

Gross, Melissa. 2000. "The Imposed Query and Information Services for Children." *JOYS* 13 (Winter): 10–17.

Gross, Melissa, Cindy Mediavilla, and Virginia A. Walter. 2016. *5 Steps of Outcome-Based Planning and Evaluation for Public Libraries.* Chicago: American Library Association.

Harwood Institute for Public Innovation. 2016. *Public Innovators Lab Guide.* Bethesda, MD.

Hennepin County Library. 2016a. "Homework Help, Sept. 12, 2016–May 25, 2017." Staff manual.

———. 2016b. "K–12 Homework Help, 2015–2016." PowerPoint presentation.

"Homework Center Goals." 2014. [Monterey County Free Libraries, California.]

"Homework Help Converted to Job Help Centers." 2009. *Library Journal* 134 (January): 17.

Huffman, Celia, and Robert J. Rua. 2008. "Measuring the Effectiveness of Homework Centers in Libraries." *Children and Libraries* 6 (Winter): 25–29.

"Instructions for Homework Helpers." n.d. [Allen County Library, Indiana.]

Intner, Carol F. 2011. *Homework Help from the Library: In Person and Online.* Chicago: American Library Association.

Jacobson, Linda. 2016. "Library Homework Centers Get Boost." *Library Journal* 62 (November): 17.

Kong, Catherine. 2016. *Homework Zone at Belle Cooledge Library* (blog). homeworkzonebelle cooledge.blogspot.com.

Kysh, Lynn. 2013. "What Can We Do? Child Abuse Prevention in Public Libraries." *CLA Insider* (April). www.cla-net.org/general/custom.asp?page=600.

"La Habra Branch Library Teen Tutors." 2006. Points of Light (April 18). www.pointsof light.org/programs/recognition/dpol/awards/3181.

Lance, Keith Curry, Bill Schwarz, and Marcia J. Rodney. 2014. "Building Brighter Futures: How Students Use and Benefit from Limitless Libraries." Nashville: Nashville Public Library. www.limitlesslibraries.org/wp-content/uploads/2014/12/ Limitless-Libraries-Full-Report.pdf.

Library Foundation of Los Angeles. 2016. "Student Zones: Final Report (2015–2016)."

Ludwig, Sarah, and Linda W. Braun. 2011a. "Homework Help in the Library: What's It All About?" *YALSA Blog* (August 11). yalsa.ala.org/blog/2011/08/11/homework-help -in-the-library-whats-it-all-about.

———. 2011b. "It's Not About the Collection: Homework Help Solutions." *YALSA Blog* (August 25). yalsa.ala.org/blog/2011/08/25/it's-not-about-the-collection-homework-help .solutions.

MacMillan, Kate. 2017. "Library Partnerships for Uncertain Times." *Knowledge Quest* (February 9). knowledgequest.aasl.org/library-partnerships-uncertain-times/.

Mediavilla, Cindy. 2001. *Creating the Full-Service Homework Center in Your Library.* Chicago: American Library Association.

———. 2015. "Student Zones Evaluation: Final Report" (July 3).

Mediavilla, Cindy, and Virginia A. Walter. 2008. "Out-of-School-Time Online Homework Help in California Libraries: An Evaluation Study." California State Library (July). www.library.ca.gov/lds/docs/LSTAOSTEvalStudy.pdf.

Meyers, Elaine. 1999. "The Coolness Factor: Ten Libraries Listen to Youth." *American Libraries* 30 (October): 42–44.

Michaelson, Judy. 2009. "Online Homework Help: Evaluating the Options." *Young Adult Library Services* (Winter): 25–28.

Minkel, Walter. 2002. "When Homework Is Good Politics." *School Library Journal* 48 (April): 39.

Moellman, Lisa, and Joan Matsalia. 2013. "SmartTALK Homework Support for Kids: Staff Guide." Cambridge, MA: Harvard Teaching and Learning Partnerships. commu- nity.harvard.edu/sites/default/files/SmartTALKStaffGuide.pdf.

O'Rourke, Brigid. 2014. "Harvard Helping the Helpers: SmartTALK Collaborates with Boston Public Library's Homework Help Program to Train Teen Mentors." *Harvard Gazette* (October 29). news.harvard.edu/gazaette/story/2014/10/harvard -helping-the-helpers.

Prospect Heights Public Library District. 2014. "Prospect Heights Library Hosts Free Homework Help." *Daily Herald* (December 5). www.dailyherald.com/article/ 20141126/submitted/141128772.

Public Library Association. 2016. "Project Outcome: Year in Review, 2016 Report." www.projectoutcome.org/annual-report.

Sager, Don. 1997. "Beating the Homework Blues." *Public Libraries* 36 (January/February): 19–23.

San Diego Public Library. 2016. "Do Your Homework @ the Library Statistics." (April 12).

Search Institute. 2017. "40 Developmental Assets for Adolescents." www.search-institute .org/content/40-developmental-assets-adolescents-ages-12–18.

Seattle Public Library. 2014. "Homework Helper Toolkit."

———. 2017. "Increase Attendance at Learning Buddies Sessions for a Total 800 Attendees While Maintaining a Total 13,200 Attendees at Homework Help Sessions." performance.seattle.gov/stat/goals/mfyh-i4i9/4q79-v3a2/hhh7-euew/view.

Shaffer, Gary. 2006. "Stop the Presses!" *School Library Journal* (July): 39–40.

Shapiro, Phil. 2017. "Libraries Have Become a Broadband Lifeline to the Cloud for Students." *Ars Technica* (March 30). arstechnica.com/information-technology/2017/ 03/cloud-changes-school-3/.

"Teacher in the Library Survey Results: Key Findings." 2014. [Chicago Public Library.]

"TIL/Homework Help Logic Model." 2016. [Chicago Public Library], Children's Services.

U.S. Department of Education and U.S. Department of Justice. 2000. *Working for Children: Safe and Smart After-School Programs.* Washington, DC: U.S. Department of Education. http://eric.ed.gov/?id=ED441579.

Van Orsdel, Lee C. (2016). "On My Mind: Creating Successful Spaces." *American Libraries* (September 1). americanlibrariesmagazine.org/2016/09/01/creating-successful -spaces/.

"Volunteer Orientation for Homework Helpers: Agenda." 2015. [Seattle Public Library] (September 12).

Walter, Virginia A. 1995. *Output Measures and More: Planning and Evaluating Public Library Services for Young Adults.* Chicago: American Library Association.

———. 2009. "Sowing the Seeds of Praxis: Incorporating Youth Development Principles in a Library Teen Employment Program." *Library Trends* 58 (Summer): 63–81.

Walter, Virginia A., and Cindy Mediavilla. 2003. "Homework Center Outcomes." UCLA Department of Information Studies. is-intranet.gseis.ucla.edu/research/ homework/.

———. 2005. "Teens Are from Neptune, Librarians Are from Pluto: An Analysis of Online Reference Transactions." *Library Trends* 54 (Fall): 209–26.

Walter, Virginia A., and Elaine Meyers. 2003. *Teens & Libraries: Getting It Right.* Chicago: American Library Association.

Warton, Pamela M. 2001. "The Forgotten Voices of Homework: Views of Students." *Educational Psychologist* 36 (Summer): 155.

Weisner, Stan. 1992. *Information Is Empowering: Developing Public Library Services for Youth at Risk.* Oakland, CA: Bay Area Library and Information System.

YALSA Board of Directors Meeting. ALA Annual Conference, San Francisco, June 26–30, 2015. www.ala.org/yalsa/sites/ala.org.yalsa/files/content/HomeworkHelp_AN15 .pdf.

# INDEX

**A**

*Academic Search Premier* (database), 54
achievement, measurement of, 75–76
Adamec, Janet, 63
Adams, Suellen S., 71, 72
*African American Experience* (database), 54
"After Hours Study Night" program, 45
after-school programs, 1–2
ALA (American Library Association), ix–x, 61
Allen County Public Library, Indiana
    expectations for homework program, 65
    homework help survey by, 10–11
    job duties of staff at, 25
    promotion of homework program, 72
American Library Association (ALA), ix–x, 61
AmeriCorps VISTA, 91
Amherst H. Wilder Foundation, 91
Angelou, Maya, 130
appendixes
    community assessment tools, 95–97
    homework helper application forms, 101–104
    homework helper contract, 105–106
    homework staff job descriptions, 107–116
    homework staff recruitment announcements, 98–100
    letter of intent, 131
    model homework programs, 82–94
    registration forms, 134–137
    staff manual excerpts, 127–130
    survey instruments, 138–158
    teacher letters, 132–133
    training modules, 117–126
application
    hiring process, 23–24
    homework helper application forms, 101–104
    *See also* recruitment
Arlington Public Library, Virginia, 45
Aronson, Marc, 53
assessment, 95–97
    *See also* community assessment; evaluation
Auerbach, Barbara, 10
Auxier, Tiffany, 45

**B**

Bailey, John F., 3
Bailey, Melissa, 89

Barack, Lauren, 38
Barnes & Noble, 55
Bartle, Susan M., 53
behavior
    disruptive, 66
    improvements with homework center, 3–4
    outcomes of library services, 73
    rules of conduct, 66–67
    Study Zone Tutoring Guidelines, 120–123
Belle Cooledge Library, California
    blog about, 77
    hiring process at, 23
    Library Homework Zone Coach Information, 102–104
    Teen Coach Application, 99–100
benefits
    *See* outcomes
Bexley Public Library, Ohio, 22
Boland, Becca, 45
"Book-a-Librarian" program, 47
books
    Common Core State Standards and, 52–53
    homework center collection development, 51–52
Boston Public Library, Massachusetts
    826Boston partnership, 33
    Homework Help Mentor Job Description, 107–108
    homework help mentors at, 20
    Homework Help program, 82–83
    mission statement of, 13
    service hours of, 43
    teacher tutors at, 20–21
Boxler, Julia, 84
Brainfuse HelpNow, 55–57
*BrainPOP*, 54
Brannon, Sian
    on funding, 32
    on homework center collection, 52
    on supplies cart, 60
    on survey for homework center, 10
Braun, Linda W.
    on computer equipment, 61
    on focus of homework help, xi
    on homework center service hours, 45
    on space for homework center, 39
    on staff qualifications, 20
    on teen input for homework center, 8

Brewer, Rosellen
    on effectiveness of homework program, 73
    observation by, 9
    on paid/volunteer staff, 20
    on Seaside branch, 3
    on starting after-school center, 7
BridgeUP program, 49
Brisson, Sarah-Ann, 42
Brooklyn Public Library, New York
    enhanced homework help, 47–48
    homework assistance survey by, 10
    "Homework Help for Kids" site, 55
    MyLibraryNYC, 38
    partnerships of, 33
Brossard Public Library, Quebec, Canada, 42
Brown, Jane R., 4
budget, 32

**C**

California
    after-school homework help programs in, 2–3
    homework centers in, 7
    online tutoring via public libraries in, x
California Library Association, 79
California State Library
    after-school homework assistance, x
    publicity for homework help program, 69
    study on online tutoring, 56
Callaci, Dorothy, 38
career centers, 49
Carnegie Council on Adolescent Development, 1
Carollton Public Library, 45
CCSS (Common Core State Standards), 52–53
Chamberlayne, Charles, 70
Chicago Public Library, Illinois
    goals for Teacher in the Library program, 14
    HelpNow, use of, 55–56
    media release, 70
    outcomes for Teacher in the Library program, 74–75
    promotion of homework program, 72
    Teacher in the Library, overview of, 83–84
    Teacher in the Library Survey: Child, 138–139
    Teacher in the Library Survey: Parent/Guardian, 140–141
    teachers as homework helpers at, 20
child abuse
    policy about, 64
    Study Zone Tutoring Guidelines, 125
Cleveland Food Bank, 34
collaboration, 35–38
collection
    best practices, 51
    Common Core State Standards and, 52–53
    development considerations, 51–52
    electronic resources, 54–55
    library collaboration with schools for, 37–38
college students, 22
Columbus Metropolitan Library, Ohio, 49
Common Core State Standards (CCSS), 52–53
communication
    collaboration with schools, 37–38
    marketing of homework center via channels, 71–72

    between schools/public library, 35–36
    skills, 4
community, partnerships with, 33–34
community assessment
    creation of library homework centers and, 7–8
    direct input, 10–11
    environmental scans/literature review, 9
    methods for, 8–9
    need for, 8
    observation, 9–10
    tools, 95–97
Community World Café discussion, 48
computer equipment, 60, 61
*Contemporary Authors* (database), 54
contracts, 105–106
corollary assistance, 49–50
*Creating and Managing the Full-Service Homework Center*
    (Mediavilla), ix–xii
*Creating the Full-Service Homework Center in Your Library*
    (Mediavilla), ix
critical thinking, 53
*CultureGrams* (database), 54
Cuyahoga County Public Library, Ohio
    Homework Center Coordinator Position Description,
        109–111
    homework center furnishings, 60
    Homework Center Mentor Position Description,
        112–114
    homework center service levels of, 15
    homework centers of, 7
    Homework Centers/Homework Mentors programs,
        84–85
    homework program of, 3
    Parent/Guardian Homework Center Survey Exit,
        142–143
    partnership of, 34
    program registration, 66

**D**

databases, 54–55
De Rosa, Cathy, 55
digital equity, 61
direct input
    for community assessment, 10–11
    effectiveness of, 8
Do Your Homework @ the Library program
    Parent Survey, 151–156
    in summer, 45
    Survey for Grades 6 and Up, 149–150
    Survey for Grades K-5, 148
    *See also* San Diego Public Library
Dunmore, Angela J., 2–3

**E**

Edwards, Margaret A., 2
Eggers, Dave, 33
826NYC
    guidelines for homework help, 65
    partnership with Brooklyn Public Library, 33
    program description, 47–48
Elam, Lynn, 45
electronic resources, 54–55

*Elements of Style* (Strunk & White), 52
Eli and Edythe Broad Foundation, 31, 70, 87
Emanuel, Rahm, 55–56, 70
English-language learners
 homework centers for, 4
 Study Zone Tutoring Guidelines, 124
enhanced homework help, 47–48
enrichment programs, 48–49
Enrichment Zones, NYPL, 48, 52–53
environmental scans, 8, 9
evaluation
 achievement, measuring, 75–76
 outcome statements, 74–75
 outcome statements, borrowing, 80–81
 outcome-based homework help programs, 73–74
 quality, measuring, 77–79
 quantity, measuring, 76–77
events
 for opening of homework center, 71
 special events/recognition, 69–70
exams, 45
expectations
 false, avoidance of, 63
 tutor expectations guidelines, 117–119
expert knowledge, 8

**F**

*A Fair Garden and the Swarm of Beasts* (Edwards), 2
Favot, Sarah, 70
feedback, 77–79
"Finals Service" program, 45
finals week, 45
First 5 California program, 40
*5 Steps of Outcome-Based Planning and Evaluation for Public Libraries* (Gross, Mediavilla, & Walter), 8
flyers, 70, 71
focus groups, 79
Fort Wayne Library, Indiana, 10–11
"40 Developmental Assets" (Search Institute), 80
Free Library of Philadelphia
 homework helpers in LEAP program, 21
 LEAP funding, 32
 LEAP program, description of, 49
Friendly Stop, Orange Public Library, California, ix
friends groups, 32
full-service homework center, xi
funding
 sources of, 31–33
 talking points, 33
furnishings, 60
furniture, 60

**G**

Garcia, June
 on computer equipment, 61
 on elements for student success, ix
 on homework help issues, 16
 list of potential partners, 34
 on space for homework center, 39
Generation Next, 34
goals
 of after-school homework program, 13–14

in outcome statements, 80–81
 for service plan, 17
grants, 31–33
Gross, Melissa
 *5 Steps of Outcome-Based Planning and Evaluation for Public Libraries*, 8
 on measurement of achievement, 75
 on partnerships, 33
 on student classification of librarians, 2
Grosser, Cort, 42
Gwinnett County Library, Georgia, 21, 72

**H**

Hardiman, Karen Cropsey, 2–3
Harvard University's Teaching and Learning Partnerships program, 29, 82–83
Harwood Institute for Public Innovation, 8
head counts, 76
HelpNow, Brainfuse, 55–57
Hennepin County Library
 funding for homework helpers, 32
 Generation Next partnership, 34
 goals of after-school homework program, 13–14
 help with college applications at, 50
 homework help site team, 19–20
 Homework Help staff recruitment announcement, 98
 homework helper staff manual, 29
 mission statement of, 13
 outcomes for homework centers of, 80
 recruitment announcement of, 22
 staff manual excerpt, 127
Hildreth, WyLaina
 on funding, 32
 on homework center collection, 52
 on supplies cart, 60
 on survey for homework center, 10
Hinsdale Public Library, Illinois, 45
hiring
 homework helper application forms, 101–104
 of homework helpers, 20, 23–24
 homework staff recruitment announcements, 98–100
 program security and, 63
 *See also* recruitment
holidays, service hours during, 45–46
homework, purposes served by, 1
homework alert form, 35–36
Homework Center Coordinator Position Description, 109–111
Homework Center Mentor Position Description, 112–114
homework centers
 after-school programs, benefits of, 1–2
 benefits of homework help programs, 3–5
 collaboration with schools, 35–38
 community assessment methods, 8–9
 creation of, 7–8
 critical elements for, xi
 evaluation/measuring outcomes, 73–81
 expectations for program, 64–65
 funding sources, 31–33
 library resources for, 51–57
 partnerships of, 33–34

homework centers (*continued*)
    program registration, 65–66
    program security, 63–64
    programming/corollary services, 47–50
    publicity for, 69–72
    rules of conduct, 66–67
    service hours of, 43–46
    service plan for, 13–18
    services, evolution of, x
    space/location for, 39–42
    staff/volunteer recruitment, 19–24
    students and public libraries, 2–3
    study of, ix–x
    supplies/equipment, 59–61
Homework Centers, Saint Paul Public Library, 90–91
Homework Centers/Homework Mentors, Cuyahoga
  County Public Library, 84–85
"homework fill rate" form, 76
"Homework Help Best Practices" (RUSA/YALSA)
    on needs assessment, 8
    on staff, 20
Homework Help, Boston Public Library
    Mentor Job Description, 107–108
    overview of, 82–83
    staff recruitment announcement, 98
"Homework Help Converted to Job Help Centers" (*Library
  Journal*), 49
"Homework Help for Kids" site, 55
"Homework Help, Parent Edition" program, 48
Homework Help, Seattle Public Library, 91–92
Homework Help Student Survey 2016, 157–158
homework helpers
    application forms, 101–104
    hiring process, 23–24
    homework helper contract, 105–106
    job descriptions for, 25
    job duties of, 26
    outcome statements and, 80
    paid vs. volunteer staff, 19–20
    recruitment of, 21–23
    relationship with students, 4–5
    responsibility for homework program, 17–18
    staff manual excerpts, 127–130
    staff qualifications, 20–21
    survey for measuring quality of program, 79
    training of, 27–29
    *See also* staff
Homework Help/Tutoring, Mission Viejo Library, 88–89
homework staff job descriptions, 107–116
homework staff recruitment announcements, 98–100
homework supplies, 59–60
"homework tips" lists, 36
"homework wars," 1
hours of operation
    *See* service hours
Huffman, Celia, 3, 7
Hunger Intervention Program, 34

**I**

incentive programs, 50
Innovation Labs, NYPL
    activities of, 53
    description of, 48–49

inputs, 14
integrated floor plans, 41–42
Internet
    computer equipment for homework center, 61
    use at homework center, tracking, 76
interviews
    for community assessment, 8
    for direct input on needs, 10–11
    in hiring process, 23–24
Intner, Carol F.
    on assessment of homework assistance needed, 9
    on *Creating the Full-Service Homework Center in Your
      Library*, x
    on electronic resources for homework center, 55
    on evaluation, 80
    on flyers, 70
    on homework alert form, 35–36
    on homework center furniture, 60
    on homework help service levels, 15
    on space for homework center, 42
    on word of mouth publicity, 72

**J**

Jacobson, Linda, 19
job duties
    of homework helpers, 25–26
    homework staff job descriptions, 107–116
    written job descriptions, 27

**K**

Khan Academy website, 55
King County Library System, Washington
    All-City Training workshops, 29
    bilingual homework helpers, 21
    communication with school, 37
    expectations for homework program, 65
    help with college applications at, 50
    hiring process at, 23
    incentives at, 50
    KCLS Volunteer Agreement, 105–106
    library communication with schools, 35
    program security at, 64
    publicity for Study Zones, 69
    Study Zone coordinator, 17
    Study Zone teacher letter, 132
    Study Zones, overview of, 85–86
    training of helpers at, 27
    user-friendly publicity of, 71
Kong, Catherine, 77
Korean-American Parents Association, 34
Kysh, Lunn, 64

**L**

La Habra branch of Orange County Public Libraries
    computer equipment at, 61
    Homework Help Teen Tutor program, 7
    incentive program at, 50
    teenager homework helpers at, 22–23
    training of helpers at, 27
Lafayette Public Library, Colorado
    homework center service levels of, 15

partnership of, 34
service hours of, 44
Lance, Keith Curry, 38
languages
    hiring of homework helpers and, 23
    of homework helpers in Study Zones program, 86
    as staff qualification, 21
    Study Zone Tutoring Guidelines, 124
LAPL
    *See* Los Angeles Public Library
*Latino American Experience* (database), 54
launch events, 69–70
LEAP
    *See* Literacy Enrichment After-School Program
learning, 27–29
"learning buddies" program, 47
*LearningExpress Library* (database), 54
"Let's Get Crammin'" program, 45
letter of intent, 131
librarians
    collaboration with schools, 35–38
    homework center space, 41–42
    observation by, 9–10
    relationship with students, 2–3
    responsibility for homework program, 17–18
library
    space/location for homework center, 39–42
    special events/recognition, 69–70
    *See also* homework centers; public libraries
Library Foundation of Los Angeles, 31, 76–77
library foundations, 31, 33
library resources
    best practices, 51
    collection development considerations, 51–52
    Common Core State Standards and, 52–53
    electronic resources, 54–55
    online tutoring, 55–57
Library Study Center, Paso Robles Library, 89–90
Limitless Libraries program, 37–38
links, 55
Literacy Enrichment After-School Program (LEAP)
    description of, 49
    evolution of, x
    funding for, 31, 32–33
    homework helpers in, 21
literature review, 9
Long Beach Public Library, California
    career center at, 49
    Family Learning Centers, funding for, 31
    service hours of, 44
    staff of, 20
Los Alamos branch, Santa Maria, California
    collaboration with schools, 37
    program registration, 65
    registration form, 134–135
    reopening of, 10
Los Angeles Public Library (LAPL)
    computer equipment at, 61
    donation for, 70
    expectations for homework program, 64–65
    funding for Student Zone program, 31
    homework centers, benefits of, 3
    homework helpers, responsibility of, 21
    mission statement of, 13

PowerMyLearning partnership, 34
The Quad, 41, 42, 60
    on scheduling homework programs, 44
    staff for Student Zone program, 19
    staff of, 20
    Student Zones information on website of, 16
    Student Zones, overview of, 86–87
    Student Zones service hours, 43
    supplies/equipment for Student Zones, 59
    survey for homework helpers at, 79
    use of Student Zones, survey on, 76–77
Ludwig, Sarah
    on computer equipment, 61
    on focus of homework help, xi
    on homework center service hours, 45
    on space for homework center, 39
    on staff qualifications, 20
    on teen input for homework center, 8

## M

Mack, Candice, 86
MacMillan, Kate, 37
magnets, 71
*Mango Languages* (database), 54
*Manual for Writers* (Turabian), 52
manuals, 29
marketing
    *See* publicity
Mary Idema Pew Learning and Information Commons, 60
math
    benefits of homework help programs, 3–4
    electronic resources for homework center, 55
    enhanced homework programs for, 47, 49
    hiring of homework helpers and, 23
    peer-tutoring service, 10
    scheduling factors, 44
Matsalia, Joan, 29
McChesney, Elizabeth, 83
MCFL Homework Center Parent Survey, 146–147
MCFL Homework Center User Survey, 144–145
media
    media release, 70
    strategy, techniques for, 71
    *See also* publicity
Mediavilla, Cindy
    on benefits of homework center, 4
    on collaboration with schools, 36
    on computer equipment, 61
    *5 Steps of Outcome-Based Planning and Evaluation for Public Libraries*, 8
    on homework center staff orientation, 28–29
    interview questions, 23–24
    on job duties of homework helpers, 25–26
    on measurement of achievement, 75
    on online tutoring, 56
    outcome statements, 80
    on partnerships, 33
    study of virtual librarians, 2
    supplies/equipment for Student Zones, 59
    on teenage homework helpers, 23
Mendieta, Toni, 93
mentoring
    BridgeUP program, 49

mentoring (*continued*)
 Homework Help Mentor Job Description, 107–108
 in SUCCESS program, 48
Metro Nashville Public Schools, 37–38
Meyers, Elaine
 on benefits of homework center, 4
 on librarians and students, 2
 outcome statements, 80
Michaelson, Judy, 56
Minkel, Walter, x
mission statement, 13
Mission Viejo Library, California
 Homework Help/Tutoring, overview of, 88–89
 program registration, 66
 registration form, 136–137
 service hours of homework programs of, 44
Mitnick, Eva, 19
*MLA Handbook for Writers* (Modern Language Association),
 52
model homework programs
 Homework Centers, Saint Paul Public Library, 90–91
 Homework Centers/Homework Mentors, Cuyahoga
  County Public Library, 84–85
 Homework Help, Boston Public Library, 82–83
 Homework Help, Seattle Public Library, 91–92
 Homework Help/Tutoring, Mission Viejo Library,
  88–89
 Library Study Center, Paso Robles Library, 89–90
 Student Zones, Los Angeles Public Library, 86–87
 Study Zones, King County Library System, 85–86
 Success, Winters Branch, Yolo County, 93–94
 Teacher in the Library, Chicago Public Library,
  83–84
Moellman, Lisa, 29
money, 31–33
Monroe County Library, Indiana
 collaboration with schools, 37
 recruitment of homework helpers, 22
 service hours of, 44
Monterey County Free Libraries, California
 funding for homework program, 31–32
 Homework Center Parent Survey, 146–147
 Homework Center User Survey, 144–145
 Homework Pals program, off-site, 40
 homework program, benefits of, 4
 library communication with schools, 35
 mission statement/goals for homework help
  program, 14
 online tutoring at, 56
 recruitment brochure of, 21–22
 service learners at, 26
 site coordinators of, 20
 teacher letter, 133
 training of helpers at, 27
Multnomah County Library, Oregon
 electronic resources of, 55
 virtual "Homework Center," 52
MyLibraryNYC, 38

**N**

Nashville Public Library, Tennessee, 37–38
National City, California, 2–3
National Honor Society, 22

Nelson, Sandra
 on computer equipment, 61
 on elements for student success, ix
 on homework help issues, 16
 list of potential partners, 34
 on space for homework center, 39
New York City Department of Education, 38
New York Public Library (NYPL)
 Common Core State Standards and, 52–53
 electronic resources of, 54
 enrichment programs of, 48–49
 MyLibraryNYC, 38
noise, 40–41

**O**

observation, 9–10
OCLC (Online Computer Library Center), 55
off-site homework help program, 40
Ojai Valley Library Foundation, 17, 32
online resources
 electronic resources for homework center, 54–55
 for homework center collection, 52
online tutoring, 52
open floor plan, 41–42
*Opposing Viewpoints Resource Center* (database), 54
Orange Public Library, Friendly Stop center, 40
orientation
 elements of, 28–29
 for homework help staff, 27
O'Rourke, Brigid, 29
outcome statements
 borrowing, 80–81
 for Teacher in the Library program, 74–75
outcomes
 accomplishment of goals as, 14
 achievement, measuring, 75–76
 outcome statements, 74–75
 outcome statements, borrowing, 80–81
 outcome-based homework help programs, 73–74
 program evaluation based on, 77
 quality, measuring, 77–79
 quantity, measuring, 76–77
 survey for, 78
outsourcing, 17

**P**

Palos Verdes Library District, California, 37, 53
Parent Survey, 95
Parent/Guardian Homework Center Survey Exit,
 142–143
parents
 corollary enrichment services for, 49
 Do Your Homework @ the Library Program: Parent
  Survey, 151–156
 expectations for homework program, 64–65
 homework help for, 48
 homework help from, 1
 MCFL Homework Center Parent Survey, 146–147
 outcomes for Teacher in the Library program, 75
 Parent/Guardian Homework Center Survey Exit,
  142–143
 program registration and, 65–66

program security and, 64
    survey for measuring quality of program, 78
partnerships
    collaborative funding for homework center, 32
    with community, 33–34
Paso Robles Public Library, California
    computer equipment at, 61
    incentives at, 50
    Library Study Center in, 40
    Library Study Center, overview of, 89–90
    Library Study Center, partnership for, 33
    program security, 64
    rules of conduct at, 66–67
    service hours of Library Study Center, 45
PhillyBOOST, 32–33
PLA
    See Public Library Association
plan
    See service plan
policy, for homework program, 16
PowerMyLearning, 34
Poyner, Annie, 69, 85
printing, 61
program security, 63–64
programming/corollary services
    corollary assistance, 49–50
    enhanced homework help, 47–48
    enrichment programs, 48–49
    incentives, 50
Project My Turn, 2–3
Project Outcome, 81
Project Understanding, 17–18
Prospect Heights Public Library District
    electronic resources at, 54
    homework helper application form, 101
    library communication with schools, 37
public knowledge, 8
public libraries
    collaboration with schools, 35–38
    homework help programs, benefits of, 3–5
    students and, 2–3
Public Library Association (PLA)
    on homework help service levels, 16
    list of potential partners, 34
    on outcomes for homework help programs, 73–74
    Project Outcome, 77, 81
    on space for homework center, 39
*Public Library Service Responses* (Public Library Association), ix
*Publication Manual of the American Psychological Association*
    (APA), 52
publicity
    communication channels, 71–72
    special events/recognition, 69–70
    strategies for, 69
    user-friendly publicity, 70–71
purpose, 13–14

for measurement of achievement, 75
    survey for measuring quality of program, 77–78
quality, measurement of, 77–79
quantitative data
    for evaluation of program, 77
    for measurement of achievement, 75
    survey for measuring quality of program, 77–78
quantity, measurement of, 76–77
Queens Public Library, New York
    homework tips at, 36
    MyLibraryNYC, 38
questionnaires, 10–11

**R**
rebranding, 51, 52
recognition, 70
recruitment
    of homework assistants, 21–23
    homework helper application forms, 101–104
    homework staff recruitment announcements, 98–100
    paid *vs.* volunteer staff, 19–20
reference materials, 51, 52
Reference User Services Association (RUSA)
    on collaborative funding, 32
    on evaluation of homework help programs, 75–76
    on homework center service hours, 46
    homework-related collection, best practices, 51
    on in-library homework assistance, ix–x
    on marketing via existing communication channels,
        71
    on needs assessment, 8
    on new homework centers, 9
    on online tutoring, 56–57
    on recruitment, 22
    on service hours, 43
    on space for homework center, 39
    on staff, 20
registration
    forms, examples of, 134–137
    for homework program, 65–66
remote homework help programs, 40–41
resources
    See appendixes; electronic resources; library
        resources
responsibility
    for homework program, 17–18
    job duties of homework helpers, 25–26
RISE, Inc.
    partnership with Winters branch library, 33
    SUCCESS program at Winters library, 17, 48, 93
Rodney, Marcia J., 38
Rua, Robert J., 3, 7
rules of conduct, 65, 66–67
RUSA
    See Reference User Services Association

**Q**
The Quad, Los Angeles Public Library
    features of, 87
    space for, 41, 42
qualitative data
    for evaluation of program, 77

**S**
Sacramento Public Library, California, 44
    See also Belle Cooledge Library, California
Sager, Don, 2
Saint Paul Public Library, Minnesota
    college students, recruitment of, 22

Saint Paul Public Library, Minnesota (*continued*)
    Homework Centers, 90–91
    mission of, 14
San Diego Public Library (SDPL)
    Assistant Management Analyst Job Description, 115–116
    Do Your Homework @ the Library Program: Parent Survey, 151–156
    Do Your Homework @ the Library Program: Survey for Grades 6 and Up, 149–150
    Do Your Homework @ the Library Program: Survey for Grades K-5, 148
    event for launch of program, 69–70
    homework center usage, tracking, 76
    homework help service hours at, 45
    homework supplies at, 60
San José Public Library, Alviso branch, 32
Santa Clarita Public Library, California
    "Homework Help, Parent Edition," 48
    mission statement of, 13
satisfaction, 78
scheduling, 43–44
schools
    collaboration with, 35–38
    promotion of homework program, 72
Schwarz, Bill, 38
*ScienceFlix* (Scholastic), 54
Search Institute, 80
Seaside Public Library, California, 3
Seattle Public Library, Washington
    All-City Training workshops, 29
    community assessment for homework centers, 9
    homework center space, 41
    Homework Help, overview of, 91–92
    Homework Help Student Survey 2016, 157–158
    homework helper at, 20
    homework helper toolkit, 29
    "learning buddies" mentors at, 47
    partnership of, 34
    quality of program, measurement of, 77
    staff manual excerpts, 128–129
    training of homework helpers at, 28
security
    procedures for homework center, 65
    program security, 63–64
service hours
    finals week, 45
    scheduling factors, 43–44
    summer/holidays, 45–46
service levels, 15–16
service plan
    purpose, defining, 13–14
    responsibility for program, 17–18
    service levels, 15–16
    talking points, 17
Shaffer, Gary, 33
Shapiro, Phil, xi, 61
site coordinator, 20
SmartTALK training, 29, 82–83
Solano County Library, 79
space
    for homework center, 39–42
    for homework help during finals week, 45
    program security and, 64

SparkNotes (website), 55
staff
    decision-making, involvement in, 34
    expectations for homework program, 64–65
    hiring process, 23–24
    homework helper application forms, 101–104
    homework helper contract, 105–106
    homework staff job descriptions, 107–116
    homework staff recruitment announcements, 98–100
    job duties of, 25–26
    location of homework center and, 40–41
    paid vs. volunteer staff, 19–20
    qualifications, 20–21
    recruitment of, 21–23
    security of program and, 63–64
    service hours of homework center, 43–46
    training of, 27–29
    *See also* homework helpers
staff liaison, 37
staff manual excerpts, 127–130
standards, 52–53
STEAM, 55
Stimson, Sarah, 88
Strunk, William, Jr., 52
Student Survey, 96
Student Zones, Los Angeles Public Library
    computer equipment of, 61
    funding for, 31
    homework helpers, responsibility of, 21
    overview of, 86–87
    The Quad, description of, 42
    service hours of, 43
    staff for, 19
    supplies/equipment for, 59
    use of program, survey on, 76–77
    *See also* Los Angeles Public Library
students
    direct input on homework center, 10–11
    expectations for homework program, 64–65
    focus groups about homework program, 79
    homework centers, benefits of, 3–5
    job duties of homework helpers, 25–26
    online tutoring and, 55–57
    outcomes for Teacher in the Library program, 74–75
    program registration and, 65–66
    program security and, 63–64
    public libraries and, 2–3
    rules of conduct, 66–67
    service hours of homework center, 43–46
Study Zones, King County Library System
    overview of, 85–86
    teacher letter, 132
    Tutoring Guidelines, 117–126
    *See also* King County Library System, Washington
"Succeed in School: Homework Help" (Public Library Association), 16, 73–74
success, 77
SUCCESS program
    description of, 17, 48
    overview of, 93–94
    *See also* Winters Branch, Yolo County, California
summer, service hours in, 45
Superhero Annex, 33

supervisors, job duties of, 26
supplies
    computer equipment, 61
    standard homework supplies, 59–60
surveys
    for community assessment, 8
    for direct input on homework assistance needs, 10–11
    Do Your Homework @ the Library Program: Parent Survey, 151–156
    Do Your Homework @ the Library Program: Survey for Grades 6 and Up, 149–150
    Do Your Homework @ the Library Program: Survey for Grades K-5, 148
    Homework Center User Survey, 144–145
    Homework Help Student Survey 2016, 157–158
    MCFL Homework Center Parent Survey, 146–147
    for measuring quality of program, 77–79, 80
    Parent Survey, 95
    Parent/Guardian Homework Center Survey Exit, 142–143
    Student Survey, 96
    Teacher in the Library Survey: Child, 138–139
    Teacher in the Library Survey: Parent/Guardian, 140–141
    Teacher Survey, 97
Szabo, John, 70

**T**
talking points
    on benefits of homework help programs, 2
    on community assessment, 8
    on corollary enrichment services, 49
    on evaluation of program, 77
    funding for homework centers, 33
    on homework center collection, 52
    on homework center supplies/equipment, 60
    on job descriptions, 27
    library/school collaboration, 37
    on media strategy, 71
    on program security, 65
    purpose of, xii
    on service hours, 44
    on service plans, 17
    on space for homework center, 41
    staff recruitment, 22
Teacher in the Library program, Chicago Public Library
    benefits of, 3
    goals for, 14
    overview of, 83–84
    Teacher in the Library Survey: Child, 138–139
    Teacher in the Library Survey: Parent/Guardian, 140–141
    teachers as homework helpers, 20
teacher letters, 132–133
Teacher Survey, 97
teachers
    library collaboration with schools and, 35–38
    staff qualifications, 20–21
    staff recruitment considerations, 22
teamwork, 4
teenagers
    homework center service hours for, 43–44
    homework center space and, 42
    as homework helpers, 4–5
    input for homework center, 8
    recruitment of homework helpers, 22–23
    service hours during finals week, 45
    See also students
text sets, 53
textbooks
    Common Core State Standards and, 53
    for homework center collection, 52
training modules, Study Zone Tutoring Guidelines, 117–126
transportation, 44
trinkets, 71
TumbleBooks (database), 54
Turabian, Kate, 52
Tutor.com, 55, 56
tutoring
    expectations for homework program and, 65
    Expectations of Volunteer Tutors, 127
    online, 55–57
    program at Mission Viejo Library, 88–89
    Study Zone Tutoring Guidelines, 117–126

**U**
U.S. Department of Agriculture, 34
U.S. Department of Education, 2
U.S. Department of Justice, 2
U.S. History in Context (database), 54
user-friendly publicity, 70–71

**V**
Van Orsdel, Lee C., 60
Veizaga, Angela, 82
Ventura County Library, California
    funding for SchooLinks program, 32
    partnership of, 34
    responsibility for homework program, 17–18
volunteers
    hiring process, 23–24
    job duties of, 25–26
    paid vs. volunteer staff, 19–20
    recruitment of homework helpers, 21–23
    staff qualifications, 20–21
    staff recruitment considerations, 22
    training of, 27–29

**W**
Wallace Foundation, 32
Walter, Virginia A.
    on benefits of homework center, 4
    5 Steps of Outcome-Based Planning and Evaluation for Public Libraries, 8
    focus groups about homework program, 79
    on homework center usage, 76
    on LEAP, 49
    on measurement of achievement, 75
    on online tutoring, 56
    outcome statements, 80
    on partnerships, 33
    study of virtual librarians, 2
    on teenage homework helpers, 23

Warton, Pamela, 1
Watanabe, Josie, 91
website, library
    digital marketing of homework center via, 71
    homework center's purpose on, 16
    link to homework center website from school website, 72
    recruitment announcements on, 22
    SchooLinks, 53
websites
    electronic resources for homework center, 54–55
    links to on homework center webpage, 52
Weisner, Stan, 69
Whalen, Eric, 90
White, E. B., 52
winter, service hours in, 45–46
Winters Branch, Yolo County, California
    partnerships of, 33
    program security, 64
    SUCCESS helpers at, 21
    SUCCESS program, 17, 48, 93–94
word of mouth, 71, 72
*The World Book Online Reference Center* (database), 54
*World History in Context* (database), 54
writing manuals, 52

**Y**
Young Adult Library Services Association (YALSA)
    on collaborative funding, 32
    on evaluation of homework help programs, 75–76
    on homework center service hours, 46
    homework-related collection, best practices, 51
    on in-library homework assistance, ix–x
    on marketing via existing communication channels, 71
    on needs assessment, 8
    on new homework centers, 9
    on online tutoring, 56–57
    on service hours, 43
    on space for homework center, 39
    on staff, 20
    on staff recruitment, 22
youth services staff, 17–18